# Healed by Divine Miracle

## LIVING DAILY IN THE MIRACULOUS

# SALLI STEWARD MELILLI

# ENDORSEMENTS

"The author presents powerful testimony steeped in Scripture. This book will build your faith and draw you closer to the Healer."

*—Dr. Sandra Morgan, Director of Global Center for Women and Justice, Vanguard University*

"As a close friend and Pastor to Jonathan and Salli for over 30 years, I was with them and witnessed Salli's miracle healing. I urge you to read this testimony of the healing power of our God."

*—Rev. Jim Rentz, Pastor at Healing Place Church & Chaplain at Angola State Penitentiary*

"Salli Melilli gives an accurate, personal account of the faithfulness of God."

*Dr. Peter Bostick, MD Hematology/Oncology & Dr. Leslie Bostick, MD Pediatrician Author of "Guidelines for Maximum Health: The Power of Faith and Medicine" (Faith One Publishing)*

"My dear friend and sister in Christ, Salli Melilli, has written a beautiful and powerful account of her life in the hands of an intimate and miracle working God. Her incredible story will create a hunger and thirst in the reader to get to know this same God and experience, as Salli has, a personal and eternal relationship with Him through Jesus Christ. Her amazing personal testimony of God's faithfulness and healing power, intermingled with solid biblical teachings, will minister not only faith for healing, but wise counsel and instruction.

As one of Salli's prayer partners, I can personally attest to the validity of her divine healing from cancer; having prayed with her during the dark and discouraging times of suffering and negative medical reports, and rejoiced with her as the healing "report of the Lord" was confirmed by her doctors!

Salli's story is one of overcoming faith, perseverance, compassion, supernatural healing, tears and gladness; along with wisdom forged in the fires of adversity. I'm honored to be able to endorse a book that will minister greatly to the body of Christ. "Healed By Divine Miracle" will surely inspire and encourage all who are blessed to read it!

*Sally Koch, Co-Founder & Chairwoman*
*of Women Praying for Women Ministries*

# ACKNOWLEDGMENTS

THERE ARE TOO many people to thank here that played a vital role in this book coming to fruition. In fact, there are many I won't even know were involved until we all get to heaven. People who prayed for my parents. People that prayed for me as a baby. People who prayed for me throughout my life. People, all over the world, who prayed for me during my journey through cancer.

There are family members, friends, and countless members of the Body of Christ who have stood with me; and for that I am eternally grateful.

I want to especially thank Paulette Beckner, Debra Miller and the "sistas" of our Transformed and Renewed Bible study group; all my prayer warriors with the Women Praying for Women group; and our "church without walls" that met in our home to pray and worship together. You know who you are and you all are such an "above and beyond" blessing to me!

To David and Darrellyn Melilli for all your love, prayers and encouraging words…and for a beautiful hideaway to work on this book!

To Steven Novak for the cover design. You had no idea, when you designed the cover, that yellow daisies were my favorite bouquet of flowers to receive during my countless hospital stays as a child!

Thank you, Rev. Jake Kail, for your advice, guidance and prayers.

Thank you KayLynn Flanders, Rachel Hebert, Debra Miller, and Dr. Leslie Bostick for all the proofing, editing, and formatting.

To my wonderful husband, Jonathan—this wouldn't have happened without your tireless love and support! I love you!

And above all else, an eternal thank you to my Lord Jesus Christ, my Healer, my Savior, and soon coming King…You are my everything!

# DEDICATION

This book is dedicated to my mother and father,

*Rev. Harold and Saundra Steward*

The testimonies contained within the pages of this book would never have been if not for their mighty faith in Jesus and their uncompromising obedience to His calling. They prayed for me relentlessly until they graduated to heaven. They are now part of that great cloud of witnesses that, I believe, are still praying for us all.

To my son and daughter,

*Jonathan "Jay" and Alexandria "Lexi"*

With all my love, this book is for you. May the testimonies contained in these pages encourage you to never stop believing and never stop fighting the good fight of faith. No matter the cost, it will be worth it all when we see Jesus face to face!

# CONTENTS

*"Bless the Lord, O my soul;*
*and all that is within me,*
*bless His Holy name.*
*Bless the Lord, O my soul, and*
*forget not all His benefits:*
*Who forgiveth all thine iniquities;*
*who healeth all thy diseases;*
*Who redeemeth thy life from destruction;*
*who crowneth thee with lovingkindness*
*and tender mercies;*
*Who satisfieth thy mouth with good things;*
*so that thy youth is renewed*
*like the eagle's."*

*Psalm 103:1–5*

*Chapter One*

# HEALED BY DIVINE MIRACLE

*"Now unto him that is able to do exceeding abundantly above
all that we ask or think, according to the power that worketh in us,
Unto him be glory in the church by Christ Jesus
throughout all ages, world without end. Amen."*

*Ephesians 3:20–21*

## A SETUP FOR THE MIRACULOUS

**M**Y YOUNG MOTHER leaned over the bathtub bathing her baby girl's deathly ill body. She poured the cool water over my little frame in a desperate attempt to bring the fever down before further damage could incur. My one year old body was racked with high fever, pain and swelling from the infection in the bladder and kidneys. In addition, the detrimental side effects of 7+ different prescription medications on such a tiny body were taking their toll.

In spite of their best efforts, I was rapidly approaching death's door. "How much longer will I have her?" Saundra thought, as tears poured from her broken heart down her beautiful, yet tormented face. "How much longer, God? Please, don't take her from me! She's only a year old!" her heart cried.

My parents, Harold and Saundra, were young pastors, just beginning their life of ministry as the lead pastors of a wonderful church in a beautiful suburb of Portland, Oregon. They were full of faith and excitement at what God was doing in their lives. The church was growing and so was their little family. They had an adorable 3 year old daughter named Terri and another on the way.

About six months after their second baby girl was born, Saundra's heart knew something was different this time. Something wasn't right. As she held her newborn in her arms, rocking me to sleep, she thought back to Terri's first weeks and she had an uneasy feeling in her gut, telling her things weren't the same this time. Desperately trying to find answers, she spent the next several months taking me to doctor after doctor yet none could explain why I was so sick with fevers.

As they prayed and asked the Lord for help, God directed her and my father, Harold, to a doctor who at last took proper interest. While visiting family in San Diego, I spiked another dangerously high fever. The doctor in San Diego was the first doctor to suggest x-rays and testing to check my urinary tract. It was then, when I was 15 months old, that they found the source of my sickness. X-rays revealed I was born without ureterovesical valves.

Ureterovesical valves are the one-way "trap doors" that allow the urine to flow into the bladder but inhibit it from returning to the ureters and kidneys. You cannot survive without the function of these valves, but I was born without them. Since I was born without these valves, the urine would backflow into the kidneys. "But that's not all," the doctor continued, "Her bladder is the size of a grown woman's and it contains a tumor the size of a large grapefruit." Consequently, when I was standing or sitting, the vertical position would cause the tumor to fall over the opening of my bladder, preventing its ability to completely empty. And so ensued the vicious cycle: the bladder couldn't completely empty but would instead send the urine back to the kidneys to destroy them. That process would then cause my body to spike 105 degree fevers in an attempt to fight off the infection incurred by this deadly cycle.

As my parents listened to the doctor's report, they felt as if their world stood still. That began a journey that would radically change all of our lives, and countless others, forever. It was a nightmare *and* a setup for the miraculous rolled into one. Perhaps you find yourself, or someone you love, facing a nightmare of tragedy and impossibility. While no one is immune from trials and hardships in life, there is hope for the most impossible of circumstances. And I am living today for the very purpose of sharing that hope with you.

I spent much of the next two years in the hospital. My Mother spent her days torn between being at the hospital with her baby and being at home, trying desperately to create some semblance of normalcy for my 4 year old sister. My father had resigned his pastorate position and taken a secular job to offset the rising medical bills.

## SENT HOME TO DIE

It was January 1966, I was almost 3 years old when, realizing they were fighting a losing battle, the doctors called a meeting with my parents to discuss the prognosis. My Mother had to go alone to the meeting that day. She described it to me like this: "For some reason, the meeting was in a small exam room in the dimly lit basement of the hospital. As I recall, it was because those particular rooms had the equipment to display the X-rays for reading. Perhaps that was why it was dim; they probably had the lights turned down in order to read the X-ray. I just remember the sober feeling I had walking into that dimly lit room. When I walked in, there were two doctors waiting for me. I could tell by their expressions that it wasn't good news. One came and stood close to me. The other took a piece of paper and began sketching a picture of kidneys. He proceeded to show me on paper the condition of your kidneys and how badly deteriorated they were. In conclusion, he looked at me and said, "I'm sorry, Mrs. Steward, but there's just nothing more we can do. Salli's kidneys will continue to deteriorate. At the very most, she may live to be 5 years of age. We're so sorry." That was it. They had exhausted every bit of knowledge they had. All medical hope was gone. I was sent home that day to die.

Shortly after bringing me home, my mother took me to the pediatrician for more medication. In a last ditch effort to save my life, the pediatrician suggested trying something that, as far as we know, had never been done before. He wanted to perform an experimental surgery, moving the ureter to a more muscular area to see if the muscles might possibly function as ureterovesical valves. They would know if the surgery was successful because I would no longer run high fevers indicating the infection from the ongoing deterioration of my kidneys had ceased. My parents agreed to the surgery knowing it was the doctors' last hope at saving my life. That surgery was performed on March 20, 1966 at The Physicians and Surgeons Hospital in Portland, Oregon. After the surgery, they knew right away the procedure was unsuccessful as I continued running 105+ fevers.

Once again, I was sent home to die. But God had a different (and spectacular!) ending in mind for this trial.

The Lord has a way of setting up the stories of the lives of His children in such a way that *He alone* will be magnified and glorified. Psalm 34:19 tells us, "Many are the afflictions of the saints, but the Lord delivers them out of them all." He uses troubles and afflictions in our lives to get us to look to Him, and for the world to see the power of God made manifest in our suffering. In John 12:32, Jesus said, "if I be lifted up from the earth, I will draw all men to myself." When God told Moses in the wilderness to lift up the stick with the serpent on it, the children of Israel would be healed of their affliction when they gazed upon it.

That was a type and shadow of Christ, having been rejected and crucified on the tree for all to behold. When we look to Him in our times of affliction and impossibility, He can do what no man can do for us, turning the impossible into a glorious spectacle of His love, compassion, and miraculous power. He shows us this all throughout scripture.

## DELIBERATELY POSITIONED FOR HIS GLORY

In Exodus 14, when the children of Israel were delivered out of Egypt, God deliberately positioned them at the edge of the Red Sea with the Egyptian army in hot pursuit behind them. The most powerful army in the world was coming after them and the Israelites had no way to fight and nowhere to run. Have you ever felt like you were in that position? The odds are stacked against you and you see no way of escape. Your circumstances are beyond your control and you see nothing but death and destruction for your future. Before God does the impossible and parts the Red Sea in front of us, to provide a way of escape, He often allows all of man's effort to be completely exhausted before showing His mighty hand of power and love to His children *and* to their enemies. And He never does it the same way twice.

## STEPPING OUT BY FAITH

During this season in our lives, my Father would come to the hospital in the evenings after work. While I was in recovery, after receiving the post-operative report that I was going to die, he went for a walk in the halls of the hospital to pray. He cried out in his grief and desperation saying, "Whatever you ask of me, Lord, I will do it. I'll walk through any open door you call me to, if you'll just heal my baby!" When he shared that prayer with my Mother, she told him, "We don't bargain with God, we do His will." After considering her words, he simply prayed, "Lord, no matter what happens, I know you've called me to ministry and I'll go through whatever door you open." His words remind me of Job's when he said, "Though He slay me, yet will I serve Him." (Job 13:15)

Shortly thereafter, he received a call from the Northern California Assemblies of God District Office. They wanted to know if he might be interested in pastoring a church in Gustine, California. He had never heard of Gustine but agreed to think about it.

"Gustine? Where is that?" he thought. My parents were both natives of Oregon but lived in Santa Cruz, California, where he attended Bible College, so while they were familiar with the state, they had never heard of Gustine. No surprise there—it was so small, it wasn't even on the map! Fifty years later, when asking Californians if they know where Gustine is, they look puzzled responding, "never heard of it." California has grown by tens of millions since 1966, and yet still, 50 years later, few have heard of Gustine. That gives you an idea of how small and insignificant it was and still is to this day! It is a little town in the San Joaquin Valley—the heart of the agricultural part of the state. It is a very small, predominantly Portuguese community and the nearest hospital was over thirty minutes away. Not only would they leave the beautiful Portland metropolis they loved so much, they would have to leave some of the best pediatricians and one of the most cutting edge hospitals in the nation.

This wasn't just about the hospital situation though. Since starting his secular job selling mobile homes, my father had done so well. He surpassed everyone in the company and was making an enormous amount of money. He was well on his way to becoming a very wealthy man. The owner of the company had offered to setup my father with his own dealership in Corvalis (a suburb of Portland). He told my father if he would do it, he would quickly become a multi-millionaire. (Just being a millionaire in those days was enormous, but a multi-millionaire was even more rare!) Considering my father's strong leadership skill, business efficacy, and financial savvy, no one who knew him doubted his ability to be highly successful. Not only would he have to take me away from excellent medical care, he would be walking away from the chance of a lifetime and no longer have the comfortable salary to cover the escalating medical costs.

## STEPPING OUT OF THE BOAT AND ONTO THE WATER

God was calling my parents out of the boat and into the realm of the impossible by removing every support system they had and bringing them to a place of complete surrender and trust in God alone. I imagine it had to be a lot like Abraham, in Genesis 22, when God tested Abraham, and told him to take Isaac up the mountain to sacrifice him.

But my Father was a man of great faith. He and my mother knew God intimately and loved the Lord with everything in them. If the Lord was calling them to Gustine, they knew there was no other option but to trust and obey. After the call from the district office, the church in Gustine called to invite my father to come preach one Sunday and to prayerfully consider pastoring their church. He graciously accepted the invitation not knowing what to expect.

My father's brother, Everett, who was living in Fresno, California, drove up to meet us in Gustine. While my father was preaching that Sunday morning, my mother, 'the beautiful lady from the big city', stood out like a sore thumb. My mother was a very glamorous, strikingly beautiful woman. Not exaggerating, she was a cross between Elizabeth Taylor and Jackie Kennedy, even being stopped at times in stores to be mistaken for them. She had beautiful, immaculately styled black hair, gorgeous dark brown eyes, a perfect smile and a figure to match. Throughout my entire childhood I was so proud to have her as my mother. Her dresses were always the latest yet classic fashions, always polished off with gloves, stockings, and high heels with a matching handbag. She was truly a stunning sight to behold; like a picture peeled from the latest Vogue. And she had a kind, effervescent personality to match.

She was surrounded that day by humble, country folk. They wore no makeup or fancy clothes. In fact, one even showed up to church in her slippers and 'housecoat', (I'm pretty sure that's code for 'nice bathrobe'!) As her handsome young husband spoke that morning, my mother sat with her brother-in-law who found the whole scene quite humorous. He was giggling and whispering funny comments to her throughout the entire service. My mother recalled, "An older man was teaching a Sunday School class in the sanctuary with an oven mitt on his hand the entire time!" It's no wonder Everett was laughing!

That afternoon they went to the local park to sit and discuss the whole situation while I slept and Terri played. They were so taken aback by the whole debacle, they agreed not stay the night, but to leave immediately following the evening service.

As the evening service opened with several hymns, my uncle slipped a humorous note to my father. The note read, "These people are like sheep without a shepherd." When my father read the note, it struck his heart with compassion not laughter. As he preached that night, God moved upon his heart, filling it with love for this precious flock. He knew it was God's will for him to accept the position as their pastor. At the close of the service, a little elderly lady approached my parents and said, "Seventeen other ministers have turned us down. Are you going to also?" He knew he couldn't do the same. God was clearly calling him to this forgotten town on the backside of nowhere. He accepted the position and they returned to Portland to sell their home and move.

My sweet mother recalls, "I thought I was going to die along with my baby. I had to leave everything I loved: my home, the beautiful city and state where all my family and dear friends lived; not to mention all the wonderful doctors we had grown to love and deeply value." Oregon is a beautifully lush, green state with snow-capped mountains filled with majestic pine trees, rivers, parks and of course, the stunning ocean coastline. It was where my parents were both born and raised.

Portland was a gorgeous, modern city with all the shopping a glamorous girl could want. The Central Valley of California, by stark contrast, is nothing but dust and flat farmland. Stinky farmland. And when I say stinky, I mean foul.

To this day, I don't like driving through the central valley on my way from San Francisco to southern California. The sulfurous fumes of slaughterhouses and overripe, rotten fruit and veggies, mixed with the lovely stench of freshly applied fertilizer hanging in the hot 100+ degree air was more than anyone wanted to bear. My mother traded her beautiful home with its spacious and beautifully landscaped backyard for a dilapidated parsonage behind the unsightly church building.

Instead of the wonderful neighbors with whom they once enjoyed fellowship, she now had no neighbors. In place of the big backyard her children would play in and the beautifully fragrant lavender tree just outside her kitchen window, there was now a littered railroad track and the aroma of the hot valley permeating through the open window. Yet, it was soon to be called home and would yield very fond childhood memories for me and even a special place in my glamorous mother's heart.

## THE POWER OF FAITH WITH OBEDIENCE

Shortly after my sister had finished kindergarten, the day arrived for us to move to California. The U-Haul truck was packed and waiting in the church parking lot as my little family gathered with the church members to pray one more time. My father was weak with hunger from fasting and praying for my miraculous healing. My mom was quite concerned for him. She wanted him to eat something to keep up his strength. He refused, telling her he would not eat until God healed their baby. The church members prayed earnestly for my healing one more time and sent us on our way with farewell tears and hugs. As my mother and sister followed behind in the car, my father drove the U-Haul with me right by his side.

As long as I can remember, my father has been my hero. I was crazy about him. No one could make me laugh harder than he could with his hilarious wit. He was a handsome blonde with a big upper body and was strong as an ox. He had a wonderful singing voice and loved to use it to worship God. Some of my fondest memories are of his bounding down the stairs of our home singing a praise song at the top of his voice, and of his and my mom's singing duets in church. He was a true worshipper and a man of prayer. I felt, as long as I had him around, I was safe.

As a young teenager, I would quietly sit outside the door of his home office to listen to his praying for the church people. He loved them like a true shepherd. Listening to him pray would fill my heart with love, peace and a sense of security. I felt such a connection to him because God had also given me the same call to ministry and placed such a deep love for the church in my heart. He had also passed on to me the heart of a worshipper. I loved to sing and as it turned out, I wasn't so bad at it.

Church was my life. When I was in eighth grade, I told my father, "I wish I could go to school one day a week and church five days a week because I learn more in one day at church than all five days at school!" I didn't go to "children's church" for long; I wanted to be in "grown up" church where I could sing, hear my father preach, and be a part of the "altar service" (the time at the end of the service that we would spend at the altar praying and seeking God). To this day, my father is one of the greatest pastors I've ever known. When he died at 61 years of age, his funeral was standing room only in the large church that he went on to pastor in the San Francisco Bay Area. People were everywhere.

Everyone loved his strong leadership and his tender shepherd's heart. In almost 30 years of pastoring Hilltop Community Church, there was never a church split or fights; just steady, healthy growth. I was so proud of him. Growing up, all I wanted to do was please him.

I believe there was a real bonding that took place between us before I was even cognizant of the fact. When I was a small baby, he would hold me with his arm straight out, I would be on my back with my head in the palm of his hand and my body resting on his forearm with my toes touching his chest. He would walk through the house, lightly bouncing me and humming the same tune every time. He told me that when I was just a few months old, he was shocked as I began humming it with him—in tune!

Like a lot of little girls, I admired my father throughout my entire childhood. He was my knight in shining armor and a shining example of the minister and worshipper I knew by age 8, that I was called to be. When I was 15 years old, he recognized and affirmed the same call of God on me that he received as a teenager.

## THE BREAKTHROUGH

As we drove the U-Haul the night we moved to California, my father continued praying and seeking God. Suddenly, when crossing the Oregon/California state line, he recalled, "It was as if the cab of that truck suddenly illuminated with the presence of God." He said, "When I looked down at you, you looked up at me through your swollen little eyes and smiled at me. I knew in that moment, God healed you!"

After arriving in Gustine, I ran no fevers. My parents were ecstatic! God had healed their little girl! After three months of no fevers or sickness, my parents made an appointment with a urologist in Turlock, CA, to check me. The doctor ordered my medical history to be sent from Portland and scheduled tests at the Doctor's Hospital in Modesto, CA. The night before I was scheduled to go to Doctor's Hospital for the tests, my mother, out of habit, came to check on me while I was sleeping. It was at night when I would normally spike the dangerously high fevers as I was in the horizontal position and the urine would return to the kidneys like a vicious killer. When she placed her hand upon my forehead, she was horrified to find that I was burning with fever. It was the only high temperature I had spiked since crossing the state line that propitious night.

Absolutely devastated, she gathered me in her arms to put me in a cool bath. Once again, the tears streamed down her face, and mine, as she poured the cold water over my little body. That night seemed like an eternity filled with despair and anger. They thought that surely this is just an attack of Satan against our daughter and her supernatural healing. "God help us! We know you healed her! Please, God, help!" was the cry of both their hearts.

The next morning, I was checked into the hospital for treatment and to begin testing. The hospital conducted all new tests and X-rays that day and we all returned home late that evening. The following morning, the phone rang. It was the urologist calling from the hospital. "Hello, Mrs. Steward. We need you to come to the hospital right away. Something isn't right. " said the voice on the other end.

"What is it?" My mother replied, "Please tell me over the phone—I'm over thirty minutes away!" (Remember, there were no cell phones in 1966.) "Well, Mrs. Steward, as we speak, I'm staring in disbelief at the tests and X-rays we took of Salli's body. We have scoured over all the medical records from the Physicians and Surgeons Hospital in Portland and we see everything that's wrong with her. But all of our new tests and X-rays show a perfectly healthy body. The only thing our tests and X-rays reveal is a scar from the surgery. We can't explain this, Mrs. Steward, but according to our tests results, you have a perfectly normal daughter!" My Mother threw the phone and exclaimed, "PRAISE GOD! SHE'S HEALED!!"

The old tests showed the destructive deterioration of both kidneys. The new tests showed two perfect kidneys! The old tests showed my bladder to be the size of a grown woman's with a tumor the size of a grapefruit.

The new tests showed a normal-sized bladder with no existing tumor! The old tests showed no ureterovasical valves. The new tests confirmed I had two perfectly functioning valves!

## THE POWER OF GOD CONFOUNDS
## THE WISDOM OF MAN

There was no natural explanation for what had happened. In order for them to insure me with a pre-existing condition, the health insurance company placed an asterisk by my name on my policy and at the bottom wrote, "*HEALED BY DIVINE MIRACLE." Even the medical establishment and insurance company had to admit that this was something only God could do! "To God be the glory; GREAT things He hath done!"

No matter what giant of impossibility you are facing today, God is bigger. Like David when he faced Goliath, keep your focus on the size of your God not the size of your enemy (1 Samuel 17). Jesus paid the sacrificial price for us to walk in healing and victory. Nothing, I repeat, *nothing* is too difficult for God. Do you believe it? When Moses felt overwhelmed by what God was asking him to do (Exodus 3), he asked God, "Whom do I say sent me?" God responded, "I AM THAT I AM." Whatever we need, HE IS! Do you need healing? He says to you today, I AM The LORD God, Jehovah Rapha, God, the Healer!

> *"Now unto him that is able to do exceeding abundantly*
> *above all that we ask or think,*
> *according to the power that worketh in us,*
> *Unto him be glory in the church by Christ Jesus*
> *throughout all ages, world without end. Amen."*
>
> *Ephesians 3:20–21*

## PRAYER

"Heavenly Father, I thank You for Your son, Jesus Christ, and the price He bore for our salvation and healing! I thank You that You promised in Deuteronomy 31:6 to 'never leave me or forsake me' and that You are my 'ever-present help in time of need' (Psalm 46:1). Help me, Lord. Strengthen my heart, my mind and my faith, as I cling to You, obey You, and trust You. Even when facing a nightmare of tragedy and impossibility, I choose to believe that You are truly able to do 'exceedingly, abundantly more than I could ask or think' as I surrender everything to You. Forgive me for believing that suffering is nothing more than something to be feared, dreaded, and endured. Help me to see the hidden treasures of Your love, power, presence, peace, provision, and so much more along this path. May the pain I am in prod me to draw nearer to You, the One who loves me intimately and calls me by name. Fill me with Your peace as I 'keep my eyes fixed on You' (Isaiah 26:3). In Jesus' name I pray. Amen."

## FOR REFLECTION AND APPLICATION

**MEMORIZE** Deuteronomy 31:6

> *"Be strong and courageous. Do not be afraid or terrified because of them, for the LORD your God goes with you; He will never leave you nor forsake you."*

**MEDITATE** on Exodus 14, Psalm 34:19, and John 12:32

> *Think about a time that God has protected, healed or delivered you and write it down. Then, share the experience with at least two people this week.*

**READ** Exodus 3, 1 Samuel 17, and Ephesians 3:20:21

> *What giant are you facing? Is God bigger? What strategy are you taking to build your faith and trust in God?*

*Notes*

*Chapter Two*

# THE RING

*"He sent His Word, and healed them,*
*and delivered them from (all) their destructions."*

*Psalm 107:20 (NASB)*

## THE NEWS SPREAD QUICKLY

MIRACLES LIKE THAT have a way of getting people's attention. Everyone was talking about it: the pastor's daughter who was born without body parts and now has them. That's really the whole purpose for God doing miracles, isn't it? To show people who He is, how much He cares, and what He is capable of doing in our lives. It reminds me of the old hymn that says:

*"It is no secret what God can do*
*What He's done for others, He'll do for you.*
*With arms wide open, He'll pardon you;*
*It is no secret, what God can do!"*

## A FRIEND THAT STICKS CLOSER THAN A BROTHER

Two years after my healing, I got on my knees and asked Jesus to come into my heart to be the Lord and Savior of my life. Some people may believe I was too young (4 years old) to understand what I was doing, but quite the contrary. No one coerced me. I was sitting in church and heard the message of Jesus. I knew that God was real and I wanted all of Him, not just my physical healing. I wanted an intimate friendship with Him. I will never forget that moment in time. It is as real to me today, almost 50 years later, as it was in that moment. He *really did* come into my heart and I was never the same. At age 6, I was baptized in water. I remember not being tall enough to see over the edge of the baptismal but I felt as tall as a giant walking out of it. God was at work in my little life. Never underestimate what God can do in and through the life of a child.

At age 8, I received the baptism of the Holy Spirit; a gift that would radically empower me even to this very day. It set my heart on fire for what impassions the heart of God: His church and the lost. By age 10, I knew I was called to be in full-time ministry and at age 12, I began teaching a Sunday School class of 3–5 year olds. I loved telling them Bible stories and praying with them. Some of their prayer requests were hysterically funny, while others were heartbreaking.

At age 14, I started a children's choir. What a joy that was! At age 15, my best friend and I, with 65 energetic kids, put on a full-production musical. One of the children's parents, who was a hard-hearted, alcoholic attorney, came the night of the production and sat in the front row to watch his little girl perform. That night, he wept through the entire performance as he heard the message of Christ. Throughout my childhood and young adult years, I continued to see God do the miraculous in myself and those around me. God continued to use the miracle of my healing as I appeared on the 700 Club and the California Tonight Show during my late teens and early twenties. I tell you all of this, not to brag about myself, but to boast in what *God* can do through each of us (2 Corinthians 10:17). Regardless of our age, when He captures our heart and is given the opportunity to "be the boss" of us, anything is possible! He took my love for Him, my little bit of musical talent and His love in my heart for the kids in that choir and used it to draw others to His heart of love for them. He took my parents' love for Him and their willingness to follow Him and "fight the good fight of faith", no matter the cost, and use it to display His love, power and glory to the world. The last thing on my parents' mind, when holding their sick and dying baby, was that God was going to heal her and use that testimony all over the world to bring hope to millions and glory to His name. I can't stress this enough: Never underestimate what God will do through you, your children or your grandchildren when you surrender yourself to loving Him and serving Him with your whole heart.

## HE LOVES YOUR HEART NOT YOUR TALENT

As I continued ministry throughout my teen years, God continued to love me and to remain faithful to me, in spite of my messups and failures. Seventeen through 21 years of age were my 'lost' years. I never stopped loving and serving the Lord passionately, but I couldn't find the affirmation I desperately needed. I had plenty of affirmation for my talent and position; but my talent wasn't me. It was a gift I happened to be born with. What I was desperately seeking was the love and acceptance of me—the me with all my imperfections. It's amazing to me how faithful and merciful God was during that season of my life. Thankfully, nothing could separate me from His love. Our intimate friendship has most definitely been the scarlet thread throughout my entire life. He was the one place where I could always run to find love, strength, mercy, forgiveness, and direction. It took years for me to grasp that God loves me regardless of my shortcomings and imperfections. I always felt no matter what I did, it wasn't good enough for my father or for the church or even for God. It wasn't until I was 22 years of age that I realized, even though I loved God with all my heart, I was seeking affirmation in all the wrong places. It didn't matter what my (earthly) father thought. It didn't matter what the church people or any other audience thought. It didn't matter what anybody thought of me. What mattered is what God thought of me. I knew how imperfect and pathetic I was and I just couldn't believe that God loved me whether or not I ever did another good deed to win His approval. He loves us unconditionally but His approval comes through Christ in us, not our work.

It was so ingrained in me that, as the pastor's daughter of a large successful church in the San Francisco Bay Area, I *had* to be perfect. The only problem was—I wasn't. I was human. So, to compensate, I held everyone at a distance and hid behind my mask of confidence. I figured if no one got close enough to see my imperfections, I couldn't disappoint them or God. There were only a couple people I let see behind the mask, but then ran from them to protect the unrealistic demands put upon me by the deception under which I was living.

My only perfection is Christ in me, but it took many years for me to even begin to grasp the reality that no matter what I did or how well I did it, my righteousness is nothing more than filthy rags anyway (Isaiah 64:6; Romans 10:3). We must live to please and honor Christ alone as He empowers us with His Spirit. The fruit of the Holy Spirit (Galatians 5:22–23) is just that—the evidence of the work of His Spirit in me, not the works of my flesh. Any goodness in me or affirmation from God was not the result of my being an over-achiever for Jesus. That goodness can only be the overflow of a life hidden in the secret place of His presence. A life that is surrendered, filled, broken like bread and poured out like wine. From my daily intimate communion with Christ through the power of the Holy Spirit, every good and perfect gift from above could flow through me. No matter who we are, what we do, or what walk of life we come from, it is not, and never has been, about who *we* are or what *we* are capable of doing. It's about being a vessel that His love and power can flow through *as we abide in His presence.* Period.

Like the apostle Paul wrote in Philippians 2:13, "…for it is God who works in you, both to will and to work for His good pleasure."

"For if anyone thinks he is something, when he is nothing, he deceives himself." (Galatians 6:3). When we look for God's affirmation (or anyone else's) through our "goodness" (our competence), we are doomed to a life of oppression and falling short of the goal. If we could win God's approval through our works then what Jesus did at the cross was for nothing. "For it is by grace you have been saved, through faith—and this is not from yourselves, it is the gift of God—not by works, so that no one can boast." (Ephesians 2:8–9NIV). His love and approval of each of us is found through our acceptance of the blood Christ shed at Calvary. What I do for God must be *because* He loves me, not because I'm trying to win His love and approval.

## THE RING AND THE SCAR: MEMORIALS TO HIS POWER

It was approximately 1966, a few months after the miraculous healing as a child, my father announced in church one Sunday morning that he would be sharing the story of my healing that night in the evening service. Monica, a precious Mexican lady, who attended the church, was so excited. She had been praying for her husband to come to Christ for many, many years. When Monica told her husband that my parents were going to be sharing that evening of the testimony of my miraculous healing, he agreed to come and check it out for himself. Upon hearing the amazing story of God's healing power, the man accepted Christ into his life as his Lord and Savior and his life was radically changed! Shortly thereafter, Monica invited us to their home for dinner.

After a wonderful homemade mexican meal, she brought my mother to another room and presented her with a gift. It was not her birthday or any special occasion, for that matter, so my mother was a little taken aback. Upon opening the gift box, her jaw dropped as she beheld a beautiful pearl and diamond ring! My mom knew this couple didn't have much money, certainly not excess enough to buy expensive gifts. But before my mother could even say a word, Monica began to explain, "Mrs. Steward, I have been saving for several years to buy this ring for myself. However, I've been praying even longer than that for my husband to get saved. Because of Pastor Steward's and your great faith and the miracle of Salli's healing, my husband finally came to Christ. I could never thank you enough for the difference you and Pastor Steward have made in our lives. I am eternally grateful. I want you to have this ring. It's very special, just like you are to us."

My Mother wore the ring almost everyday. Every time I looked at it, I was reminded, not only of what God had done for me, but the salvation of others as a result. As a teenager and young adult, she would let me wear it on special occasions.

That ring reminded me of what Abraham (Genesis 12:7), Aaron (Exodus 32:5), Jacob (Genesis 35:7) and so many in the Old Testament would do when God had heard their prayers and provided miraculously. They would build a memorial to remember and commemorate what God had done for them. This ring stood as a memorial, a continual reminder that my God was truly able to do exceedingly abundantly more than we could ask or think according to His power that works in us (Ephesians 3:20). Furthermore, whenever someone would compliment my mother or myself on the ring, it gave us an opportunity to tell them of God's amazing grace, love, and power!

On my wedding day, my Mother gave me the pearl ring. To my horror, it was stolen from our hotel room while on our honeymoon. The ring, a memorial that had stood as a constant visual reminder of what God had done, was gone forever. The only thing left to serve as a visual reminder was the huge scar on my abdomen, and that certainly wasn't something I would be putting on display for the public to see! But unbeknownst to me, the ring being stolen was all part of God's plan to continue to work the miraculous in my life. God had an even bigger plan for that little ring; one that would completely blow my mind and catapult my faith.

The older I get, the more amazing it is to see how God uses the big and small events in our lives to bring glory to His awesome love and power. He'll seize every opportunity to reveal Himself to us if we are just willing to lay down our own agenda to see and to hear Him in the unexpected. His ways are too wonderful for our finite minds to comprehend.

> *"'My thoughts are nothing like your thoughts', says the LORD.*
> *'And my ways are far beyond anything you could imagine.*
> *For just as the heavens are higher than the earth,*
> *so my ways are higher than your ways*
> *and my thoughts higher than your thoughts.'"*
>
> *Isaiah 55:8–9 (NLT)*

In my limited understanding as a child, I couldn't understand why God had me go through a surgery that would do nothing to correct or heal my body but leave my abdomen scarred for life. But that surgery and its scars would serve as a catalyst throughout my life to point doctors to the miraculous power of God. When my parents took me to the hospital in Modesto, California, there was no doubt in those doctors minds what the doctors in Portland, Oregon had attempted to do surgically but were unable to accomplish. There was also no doubt that (by the medical staff running all new tests and X-rays) it proved my healing to everyone, even prompting the insurance company to write on my insurance record, "HEALED BY DIVINE MIRACLE". Just like Jesus, our scars can be the avenue through which Christ shines His beauty through our ashes. What was impossible with man (only leaving scars in his wake), is possible with God (leaving His light of hope to shine through the darkness of the impossible)!

During a laparoscopy in 1989, my OB/Gyn, Dr. C. Schwartzenburg, was able to see where the doctors had performed the experimental surgery back in 1965. He asked me before the surgery if he could take a look around the area (where the doctors had attempted to move the muscles) as well as examine the ureter valves. After the laparoscopy, he told me how, upon investigation, he could see the doctors' attempt to save me but it was quite clear that God had given me valves after man's failed attempt. Dr. Schwartzenburg was able to internally see the miracle of how God had healed and given me the ureterovesical valves I was born without! (I wish they had the technology back then for him to video record his investigation!) He was also able to see the extensive scar tissue left behind. He told me it was quite probable that I would be unable to carry a baby full term because of the severe scar tissue left behind from that experimental surgery performed on my little, two-year-old body. Performing my prenatal care and delivering my first child served as another testimony of the miraculous power of God to that OB/Gyn. Throughout my life, every time I have gone to a doctor I have been able to share the story of my healing.

## LIVIN' ON A PRAYER AND A PROMISE

Just like the scar on my body, that pearl ring was going to continue to point to the miraculous in ways I could have never imagined. After nine years of pastoring and planting churches in California, we decided it was time for a change. The rigorous schedule and pressure of raising small children, homeschooling intermittently, and bi-vocational church planting with chronic health issues finally caught up with me. I loved burning the candle at both ends but, unfortunately, my body wasn't designed for that. When I was a young adult, I told my mother, "the two things in life that are the biggest waste of time to me are eating and sleeping. Why would I want to sit or lie down that long when there is so much life and adventure to embrace!" I thought it was so cool that when I get to heaven, I'll have a glorified body that never tires and needs to stop and sleep. But now, as a high energy, very passionate, and driven wife, mother and minister, (who loved what I was doing!) I took on too much responsibility at the expense of my health. To all my fellow driven, perfectionistic, over-achievers reading this, I can see your head nodding up and down in true "Yep, I get ya" fashion. Most moms understand how incredibly easy it is to neglect self-care in lieu of caring for our children, husbands, careers, homes, extended family, church commitments...and on and on the list goes. Sleep was optional. Diet consisted of grabbing whatever meals were quick and easy because after all, who has time for healthy meal prep, right?! And forget 'mental health days' when you're 'loving God by serving others'! You get the picture. I was passionate, full of vigor, and headed right off the side of the health and wellness cliff. And when I fell, I fell hard (in true type A form!). [Note: Thankfully, through it all, I finally came to realize just how important boundaries, healthy diet, and sleep are.]

Of course the enemy's favorite pastime is roaming the earth, looking for those who are vulnerable to deception, that he may come in and wreak havoc in our lives. And that's exactly what he did with me. I remember one night in particular when I fell hook, line, and sinker to his coy deception. I was standing at the kitchen sink after dinner, doing dishes and feeling as if I could just slink down right there on the kitchen floor and sleep for a month. While thinking how much I needed some time away to rest, the following thought came to my mind, "You're a laborer for Christ and this is your season to work. When you get to heaven you will enter your eternal rest and be richly rewarded for not growing weary but pressing through to the end. God is pleased with all you're doing for Him and He will give you the strength to keep going."

That sounds quite noble, doesn't it? But it was certainly not of God. In fact, it sounds a lot like how Satan tempted Jesus in the wilderness and Adam and Eve in the garden. Satan hits us right in the heart of our most noble desires—to obey God and to be like Him. Thank God, for our Savior, Jesus, who wasn't deceived and didn't succumb to Satan's ploy! (And might I add here: even Jesus, who was fully God, took time to rest. He even slept while on a little boat in the middle of a very exciting, albeit scary, storm! Hmmm. Lesson learned.) However, in my desires to please God and not let anyone down, I bought the lie. Rather than taking time off, I kept going...and going. This led to a complete physical breakdown.

The doctors didn't know what was wrong with me. As my kids described it, I "went from Supermom to Super-pooped"! My body was so wracked with pain that I could barely walk or even turn a doorknob. I was down to only one pair of shoes that I could walk in without intolerable pain. (And yes, that in itself is a travesty—and all the women said, "Amen!") I went from being a light sleeper who didn't sleep much, to falling asleep on the sofa, in the middle of the afternoon, with a buzz of activity all around me, and not waking until the next day. No one could believe it! In addition, my mind had become like that of an elderly person with severe dementia. Someone would tell me something and I would turn right around and not remember anything they said. My family was concerned that I was losing my memory and possibly dying. The doctors tested me for everything from Lyme Disease to Multiple Sclerosis.

After crying out to the Lord for answers to what was happening, a friend of a friend gave me the contact information of a wonderful Christian Ob/Gyn they highly recommended. (My memory was so bad when I went to her that, to this day, I have no recollection of her name or even where her office was located!) This doctor (a godsend) was the first to diagnose me with severe Adrenal Fatigue. Adrenal Fatigue was virtually unheard of in 2006 when the diagnosis was given to me. Unfortunately, there's no quick cure for recovery. In the doctor's words, "It took you years of neglecting yourself to get to this point, and it's going to take you years of caring for yourself to recover." She was right. But it was not only the beginning of a long road to recovery, it was also the beginning of a "perfect storm" that was about to hit our little family.

Shortly after my diagnosis, Jonathan and I resigned from the church, from his second job at a Christian radio station and my second job as an adjunct professor. We said a loving and tearful goodbye to our church and family members living nearby, and moved to take a promising job out of state. I was looking forward to being able to settle in to this new chapter of our lives and continue my recovery process.

Once we arrived, my job didn't pan out as expected. Within a short time, my husband's new job took a tragic turn and ended unexpectedly. We found ourselves out of work and smack in the middle of the big 2008 recession. No, there were no moral failures and neither of us ran off with the secretary. Sometimes, like Joseph, bad things just happen to good people. And my husband is one of those really good people. He is one of the most humble, loyal men of integrity I have ever known. He loves God and he loves people. And he's always kept it that simple. Those were dark days for us. We lost everything. But God never abandoned us.

The day Jonathan came home and told me he lost his job, we sat together for quite a while in shock and disbelief. We were devastated and felt betrayed and abandoned. The grief I felt that night was the same as the grief I felt when my father, my hero, died. I remember going into my bedroom, falling on my face in desperation and crying out to God. We had done our best, but our best efforts now lay at our feet in a pile of ashes. But much like Joseph, Moses, Naomi, Daniel (and the list goes on), God was in control and was working a greater good in and through us. As I laid there weeping on the floor of my bedroom, I cried out to the Lord, "I need a word from You, God!" In my gut I knew that this trial was not going to be short, but a long, intense battle. I wept before the Lord in prayer for a long time and then opened the Bible to a passage the Lord led me to:

> *"But the LORD watches over those who fear Him,*
> *those who rely on His unfailing love.*
> *He rescues them from death and*
> *keeps them alive in times of famine."*
>
> *Psalm 33:18–19 (NLT)*

As I read that passage, He spoke to my heart, "Don't worry, I will keep you alive in this time of famine and your family will have more than enough." The peace of God flooded my heart at that moment. Even though I was hurt, devastated, and had no idea how we would make it, I had an unshakable confidence that God had spoken His word to me and that 'our God would supply all of our needs' (Philippians 4:19) and 'we would not be forsaken nor would we have to beg for anything' (Psalm 37:25). I also held to the hope and promise that "No weapon formed against you shall prosper and every tongue that accuses you in judgment, God will condemn. This is the heritage of the servants of the Lord and their vindication is from me (God)" (Isaiah 54:17).

Nothing Satan hurled at us was going to prosper! This is the unshakable joy and peace that we possess for those who are in Christ. No matter what our circumstances, God is bigger. And He promised to 'never leave us nor forsake us' (Deut. 31:6). If you've ever lost your job (or source of income) with nothing to fall back on, or felt abandoned and alone, these words are even more powerful and comforting in those seasons. Even if we're the one in the wrong, when we come to God, the Father, with a humble, repentant heart, we are met with His mercy, forgiveness, and His loving hand of comfort and provision. We cannot lose when we are in covenant relationship with God Almighty!

As pastors, we didn't have much to begin with, so it didn't take long before all our savings were exhausted. There were many days and nights (during this 2 1/2 year period) that we didn't know how we would even buy food, much less keep the water and electricity turned on. We were down to one old car, but it still managed to get us wherever we had to go. The house was for sale, but no offers were coming in and we (like so many during that recesion) lost our home. Despite our best efforts, life certainly wasn't turning out the way we thought it would. But God provided for every need we had. Throughout the entire ordeal, we always had a roof over our heads, clothes on our backs, food to eat, and 'more than enough to keep us alive.'

Though I know these programs serve a wonderful purpose for many in need, we never received welfare or food stamps. We felt we were to trust God alone for our provision. We saw miracle after miracle of supernatural provision during that season. I could write an entire book on all that God did. During an exceptionally cold winter, our central heat stopped working. At night, the outside temperature was down to 30 degrees. We were so cold but told no one. We bundled up and slept under extra blankets, but the cold was unrelenting for days. Then, one morning, I heard something at the front door. I opened the door to find 2 boxes on the porch. It was space heaters! The following summer, when hurricane Gustav hit, our neighborhood lost power for over a week. The heat and humidity were intolerable. But God sent a wonderful pastor friend to check on us. He set up an A/C window unit and generator (even filled it with gas) so the master bedroom would be cool enough for all of us to escape to. These miraculous provisions happened continuously throughout this 'time of famine'. God would send the right people at just the right times to help us, encourage us, and just be there for us. But He, was the one who remained closer than even friends and family. In the midnight hours, He was there to hold us as we grieved and cried. His precious Holy Spirit comforted us when no one else could.

## SURROUNDED BY A CLOUD OF WITNESSES

In spite of where we found ourselves, the call of God to preach the gospel and to minister to others was still burning within me "like fire shut up in my bones". I thought many times, through this season, about young Moses and how he must have felt when he tried to help his people and it all went terribly wrong. As a result, he was forced to flee Egypt and live on the backside of the desert for 40 years (Exodus 2:11–25). He had never lost his love and desire to see his people freed from slavery but his life took a devastating turn in what seemed like the wrong direction. I thought about Joseph with his coat of many colors and the dream in his heart that God had given him as a child. No matter what Joseph did right, it always seemed to blow up in his face (Genesis 37). I thought about Daniel. Daniel continued to live with integrity before the Lord even though he was taken from his home, forced to serve a foreign regime and eventually thrown into a den of lions for doing nothing wrong (Daniel 1–6). I thought of the three Hebrew children (Shadrach, Meshach and Abednego) in Daniel 3:1–30. They refused to compromise their loyalty to the one true God and were thrown into the fiery furnace for not conceding truth. They were all types and shadows of Jesus and His disciples; being rejected and yet they overcame in faith, obedience, humility, and steadfast faithfulness. Therefore, God fulfilled great and mighty exploits in and through them. (Of course, Jesus was the only one who was sinless, sent from God, and was God.)

From the time I was a child, my heart burned with a passion to see the church strong in spiritual maturity and love for one another and for the lost and hurting. Pastoring, counseling, preaching, teaching, leading worship, praying with the hurting, etc. had always been my passion. I felt so alive whenever I was able to help others in their journey to Christ and spiritual maturity. I had dreams and visions of the church serving selflessly by "loving the unlovable" rather than playing church with "a form of godliness" and piously looking down their holier-than-thou noses at those who didn't measure up to their standards. Like so many throughout Scripture, I felt that we were in our prime to do all God had called us to do, only to be cast out to the backside of the desert. But that was precisely part of His plan.

## HIS EYE IS ON THE SPARROW…AND MY RING!

While in the middle of this season of no employment, health problems, and my little family facing unthinkable heartache, I began thinking about the pearl ring stolen on my honeymoon. Just like our leadership position in the church, at a high point in my life, the ring was stolen from me. As I was pondering this, I felt prompted to search on eBay for the ring. I thought it was a futile, silly attempt but decided to just do a search to see. To my utter amazement, there it was! Could it be my ring? 'Surely', I thought, 'it must be a look-alike.' Although I had never seen another ring just like mine, I couldn't imagine a ring that was stolen over 20 years earlier, showing up on eBay at the same time that I decided to look. I was shaking all over as I carefully studied the photos of the ring. I knew I was looking at the ring from my childhood! I immediately called my mother and emailed her the pictures to examine. She had the same reaction as I. She began to tremble all over and her heart beat harder and faster as she looked at the pictures. "I really think that's it!" she said over the phone. I ordered the ring and could hardly wait for it to arrive. When it arrived, I examined the ring carefully and I had no doubt it was the ring. It was exactly the same, even down to the little imperfection in the gold setting. As I sat there holding that ring and examining it in disbelief, the Lord spoke so clearly to my heart,

"Nothing is ever too lost or too far gone that I cannot restore it to you. I always knew right where that ring was; and at the appointed time, I've returned it to you as a sign that I will restore, in due season, what the locusts have eaten in your life and the lives of your family members." (See Joel 2:25)

Wow! Like the master artist that He is, God weaves the events of our lives like a beautiful tapestry. As the threads of a tapestry intertwine to display a masterpiece, the events of my life have supernaturally and gloriously intertwined to display His love and power for all to see. For most of my life, I saw this tapestry from the back side. My life just seemed to be a series of crazy events, much how the backside of a tapestry looks. There didn't appear to be any rhyme or reason. You may feel the same about your life. You may look at it and just see a big mess. It may appear to you as the backside of a tapestry where the events seem ugly, tangled, chaotic, and random. If we're honest, many times that's also what we see when we look at other people's lives. But God specializes in taking the chaotic, tangled mess of our lives and weaving a masterpiece from it when we surrender it to

Him. Life is full of ups and downs, gains and losses, sweet moments and fiery trials, belly laughs and sobbing with groans that cannot be put into words. But through it all, I have found the loving arms of God open and waiting to hold me and comfort me whenever I run to Him and surrender my heart and life to His sovereignty. Because of the love and power of God working in his life during the worst and best of circumstances, the Apostle Paul was able to pen these words that ring so true to those in Christ:

> *". . . I have learned to be content whatever the circumstances.*
> *I know what it is to be in need, and I know what it is to have plenty.*
> *I have learned the secret of being content in any and every situation,*
> *whether well fed or hungry, whether living in plenty or in want.*
> *I can do all this through Him [Christ] who gives me strength."*
> *Philippians 4:11–13(NIV)*

That has been my personal experience as well. And perhaps yours. I've been chronically and terminally ill; given no hope by doctors. I've felt misunderstood, judged, blackballed, and abandoned by allies and enemies alike. But God has never abandoned me. Unlike the enemy, He's never lied about me or to me. Jesus walked this road of suffering before me. And He was right there with me, through it all, holding me, comforting me, providing my every need, purifying my heart, and being that "friend that sticks closer than a brother" (Proverbs 18:24). As long as I cling to the Word of God and continue to worship Him for who He is, He heals me, forgives me, refines me, covers me, and fills me with love, joy and peace—even in the worst of circumstances.

Let me encourage you to do the same. Turn on some Christian worship music, open your Bible, and pour out your heart to God. He will meet you in that place of solitude with Him and your heart will be renewed. You don't have to walk your road of suffering alone. He did that for you. Jesus was rejected, abandoned, condemned, horrifically abused, and brutally murdered by His enemies, by the religious leaders who should have lovingly received Him, and by every one of us who have sinned. But He did it for you, for me, and for all who will open the door of their hearts to Him. He bore our sin, and the wrath of God upon our sin, so that we could experience freedom, healing, and a personal relationship with God, the Father. He loves us and cares for us more than we could ever comprehend. Even when there's no one else to blame but our own selfish ambition and stupidity, He is right there with His outstretched hand of mercy. So take some time right now and write down the miracles you've experienced in your life. Write down the blessings in your life. Yes, on a piece of paper and in your smartphone, make a list of the miracles and blessings in your life and thank the Lord for each one as you name them aloud one by one. Write down the promises in Scripture (see the scripture promises in chapter seven). Read Philippians 4:4–9 and do what it says…today. Right now. He will meet you there. And regardless of your present circumstances, He will lift you out of your pit of despair and seat you at His right hand (Ephesians 2:6). And you will find yourself walking on the water with Him instead of drowning in your circumstances.

## PRAYER

"Heavenly Father, I thank You that it is by grace I am saved, through faith in Christ Jesus and not dependant on my own good works. Forgive me for underestimating what You will do through me when I surrender myself to loving You and serving You with my whole heart. Please lift me from this pit of despair and set me on the solid foundation of Jesus Christ. Holy Spirit, flood my heart and mind with peace, joy, and strength. I thank You that You are the God who heals, restores and watches over those who fear You and rely on Your unfailing love (Psalm 33:18). There is no limit to Your wisdom, love and power. Give me eyes to see Your goodness, ears to hear Your loving voice, and a heart to receive and obey Your Word. In Jesus' name I pray. Amen."

## FOR REFLECTION AND APPLICATION

### MEMORIZE Philippians 4:19

*"But my God shall supply all your need according to His riches in glory by Christ Jesus."*

### READ Psalm 37:25, Isaiah 54:17, and Philippians 4:19

*Write down the miracles you've experienced in your life. Write down at least 10 blessings in your life. Then thank God (aloud) for each one as you name them one by one.*

### MEDITATE on Philippians 4:4-13

*Paul was in prison (again) and beaten (again) for preaching about Jesus when He wrote this passage. How do your thoughts affect your emotions? In verse 4, how often did Paul say to rejoice? In verse 6, how does he tell us to offer our request to God? What will be the result (verse 7)? What did Paul say would be the result of obeying verses 8–9?*

*Notes*

*Chapter Three*

# THE GREATEST MIRACLE OF ALL

*"Jesus Christ is the same yesterday, today, and forever."*
*Hebrews 13:8*

THE BIBLE CONSISTENTLY expresses the immutable, unchanging character of God. It is crystal clear throughout scripture that God never changes.

*"Every good and perfect gift is from above,*
*coming down from the Father of the heavenly lights,*
***who does not change like shifting shadows."***
*James 1:17 (NIV)*

*"In the beginning was the Word, and the Word was with God, and the Word was God. He was with God in the beginning."*
*John 1:1–2*

*"For all the promises of God are "yes" in Christ…"*
*2 Corinthians 1:20*

It's pretty clear just from these scriptures (and there are many more to support the fact) that our God ***never*** changes. He is the great

"I AM". His very name, found in Exodus 3:14, denotes a position of permanent continuance. His actions support this claim. He healed the sick and dying in the Old Testament. He healed the sick and dying in the New Testament. And He heals the sick and dying today!

Those who claim that miracles of healing were only for the "Bible times" don't know the God of the Bible. Healing isn't **what** he **does**; it's **who** He **IS**! His **name** is "**Jehovah Rapha**" which means "The Lord that heals" (Exodus 15) "*Jehovah*" means "*The existing one; The Lord; a God who reveals Himself continually*". "**Rapha**" means "*to heal; to restore; to make healthful*". He **IS** the same yesterday, today and forever! He was Jehovah Rapha to the Israelites in the wilderness (Exodus 15) and He is Jehovah Rapha, the Risen Christ today, and "..by His stripes **WE ARE HEALED**" (Isaiah 53:5–6). He paid the price for my healing. The suffering Jesus endured leading up to His death was not just for our salvation. Being sacrificed (crucified) was the penalty for our sins that we may be reconciled to God (saved). In the old covenant, the animals were quickly and humanely killed and sacrificed for the penalty of sin. The animals were never tortured. Jesus endured the mocking and torture not only for our salvation but for our *physical healing*. In Isaiah 53:3–4, the Hebrew word for "*grief*" is "*choli*" (v.3) and "*cholayenu*" (v.4) which come from the same root word "*chalah*" which means "*sickness*" (*malady, anxiety, calamity—disease, grief (is) sick(ness)*). The Amplified Version of Isaiah 53:3–4 explicitly defines the meaning of the original hebrew text:

> *"He was despised and rejected and forsaken by men, a Man of sorrows and pains, and acquainted with **grief and sickness**; and like one from whom men hide their faces He was despised, and we did not appreciate His worth or have any esteem for Him. Surely He has borne our **griefs (sicknesses, weaknesses, and distresses**) and carried our sorrows and pains (of punishment), yet we (ignorantly) considered Him stricken, smitten, and afflicted by God (as if with leprosy)."*

The Bible says He was tortured so severely, that He was literally beaten beyond recognition.

*"But many were amazed when they saw him.*
*His face was so disfigured he seemed hardly human,*
*and from his appearance,*
*one would scarcely know he was a man."*

Isaiah 52:14 (NLT)

## I REFUSE TO LET HIS SUFFERING BE IN VAIN

When I was diagnosed with late stage ovarian cancer, I read many of these scriptures. I then came across a picture of Jesus, slumped on the ground naked, beaten and bloody with the crown of thorns pressed into His brow. As I looked at that picture, realizing He did all of that for my healing, a tenacious warrior rose up within my spirit. I held the picture up toward heaven, looked up with tears in my eyes, and said aloud to God, "I WILL NOT LET THIS BE IN VAIN!" He is *our* Healer **today**! Far be it for us to let what He suffered for our healing be squandered by ignorance, apathy and unbelief. When I was so weak and sick with cancer and chemo, I refused to give in to it. No matter how badly I felt, I would think of Jesus' horrifically bloodied, beaten body. I would start quoting the Word (even if it was just a weak whisper), *"I will not die but live and declare the works of the Lord"* (Ps. 118:17). *"He sent His Word and healed them, and delivered them from all their destructions"* (Ps.107:20). *"... by His stripes I am healed"* (Is. 53:5). No matter how weak I was, I made myself speak the verses aloud, not just think them. Remember, the power is in the *spoken* word (*"The power of life and death are in the tongue"* Pr.18:21). Even if all I could get out was a whisper, I declared the Word and resisted the sickness with my mouth from my heart. I refused to give in (to the disease) for the sake of the glory due Him.

Jesus Christ, the earthly manifestation of God Himself, bore the penalty for our sin *and* sickness at Calvary. The same God who spoke the world into existence and upholds it by His Word, is the same God who was stripped and mocked; had an entire crown of sharp thorns thrust into His head; His beard ripped from His face; and was spat upon and beaten beyond recognition. Who, then, under the weight of His cross pressing into the ripped, gouging wounds on His back and shoulders, walked the Via Dolorosa—the walk of shame—to Calvary. Once He made it to Calvary, He had nine-inch nails hammered into His hands and feet. Finally, to fulfill prophecy, they stabbed Him in His side with the sword of a Roman soldier. But the physical torture, mental and emotional taunting, the cross, nor the grave could keep Him down. He rose from the dead on the third day as the victorious King of all Kings; conquering death, hell, and the grave (Rev. 1:18)!

He's also the same God who, in 1965, gave me body parts I was born without, in 1996 healed me of chronic pain, in 2015 healed me of cancer, and in 2016 healed me of hypothyroidism. He's the same God that instantly healed my son of the flu in 1999 and delivered him from severe mononucleosis and mono-induced hepatitis in 2007. He's the same God who instantly healed my daughter from mononucleosis in the fall of 2013. She was bedridden for over two months when God instantly healed her and raised her up. I could go on and on with the miracles I have personally experienced and witnessed. I've seen the blind eyes opened and the lame walk.

As a teenager, I was in a car, sliding on black ice toward a cliff when my mother put her hand on the dash and yelled, "JESUS!" The car instantly came to a dead stop *on* black ice, saving us and our car from plunging off the edge of an Oregon cliff. I could continue telling of countless miracles I have personally received and or witnessed in others' lives; but there is still nothing more miraculous than seeing the spirit of a man completely transformed by the power of salvation in Christ.

*"In the beginning was the Word; and the Word was with God and the Word was God... And the Word became flesh and dwelt among us..."*

*John 1:1,14*

*That flesh, "...was wounded for our transgressions, was bruised for our iniquities. The chastisement for our peace was upon Him and by His stripes (wounds) we are healed."*

*Isaiah 53:5*

Jesus Christ's work at Calvary was so much more than merely providing a way for us to just make it to heaven when we die. If that's all we get from it, we've missed the whole point of the cross!

Why would the God of this universe strip Himself of all the glory, majesty, power and authority of heaven to come to this earth in the lowest path of humility? Why would He limit Himself only to the power and authority God the Father would release through Him by the Holy Spirit? Why would He choose to live on this earth as a homeless man with no job or wealth to bring Himself honor and security? No wife to support and console Him and no children to love and serve Him and bring joy to His heart? John 5:19 says implicitly, He did nothing of His own choosing, but *only* what the Father told Him to do. Why would He, the Creator of all things, the absolute treasure of heaven, submit Himself to the ridicule and rejection of pious, self-righteous, self-serving men? Why would He, the perfect Son of God, the embodiment of omnipotent purity and perfection, willingly take all the sin and shame of man upon Himself? Why would He take upon Himself the wrath of God the Father for our sin, when He never did anything to deserve it? He chose to have the bitter cup of God's wrath (toward sin) be poured out upon Himself at Calvary, that He may, in exchange, offer the cup of forgiveness and fellowship with God to us. He knew His momentary suffering would work for our eternal benefit. This is the cup we may now drink of for all eternity! He loves us that much! I love how Dr. John Piper expressed it:

*"Jesus drank the cup of God's wrath for us so that He could extend the cup of God's fellowship to us. It might include suffering, but not wrath. We don't get wrath anymore—now we get God.*
*We get the sweet, satisfying reality of His eternal fellowship in Jesus Christ, through the Holy Spirit.*
*This is the cup we drink now and forever. This is the cup that we offer those who don't know Him yet, imploring them in God's mercy, Come, drink this cup with us because Jesus drank that cup for us."*

God (the Father, the Son and the Holy Spirit—three in one) loves you more than your finite mind can comprehend and He desires an intimate friendship—even sonship—with you. He's the ultimate loving Father who would do whatever it takes to provide for His child. Unlike a flawed earthly parent, He is the omnipotent, omniscient, omnipresent, pure, and undefiled God. Jesus is the perfect brother, who out of the love for the Father, willingly laid down His life to share His throne with us; to enable us to be joint-heirs with Him. He's the Holy Spirit, who loves us enough to be an ever-present source of comfort and power in our time of need. He's the same God who created all things to be held together and function healthfully and harmoniously by His Word. And He's the same God who provided all that we need to function in a healthy, harmonious relationship with Him and with one another.

The love of God the Father toward man is first recorded in the book of Genesis. In Genesis 1, God *spoke* everything into existence, except for man.

*"And the LORD God formed man of the dust of the ground, and breathed into his nostrils the breath of life; and man became a living soul."*

*Genesis 2:7*

He made man with His own hands. Genesis 1:26 says He formed man in His image or likeness. Then He breathed His very breath of life into us! Just as a mother's body reproduces a precious life from her and the father's seed, producing a child with their DNA, looks, personality traits, etc., so God was reproducing after Himself; creating man in His image. He's still doing that today.

*"For You created my inmost being; You knit me together in my mother's womb.*
*I praise You because I am fearfully and wonderfully made;*
*Your works are wonderful, I know that full well.*
*My frame was not hidden from You when I was made*
*in the secret place, when I was woven together*
*in the depths of the earth."*
*Psalm 139:13–15 (NIV)*

Jeremiah 1:5 says He knew us before we were even in our mother's womb. Just as a new mother and father hold their newborn with awe and wonder at what their love has created, so God held the dirt in His hands and with all the love in His heart, He created a child for Himself; a child He could love and who would love Him of his own free will in return. Father God, with His own hand, created a beautiful, perfect garden for His child to live in and enjoy. He even gave him the perfect mate so that he would have another human to complete him; one whom he could enjoy and love, just as God Himself would enjoy and love their fellowship with Him. Adam and Eve were the joy of His heart.

## THE CONSEQUENCE OF LOSING FOCUS

But sin came into that garden. When Eve heard the serpent's eloquent sales pitch, she was all in. When she pitched it to Adam, they were both hooked on the proposition of being even more than God created them to be. The temptation to no longer just be what God created them to be, but to be 'like God' was just too good to pass up. The thought may have crossed their minds, as it does so many times when facing the temptation to rebel against God's commands: "I'm sure it's okay. God is a good guy; He won't mind just this once. It's not like we don't love Him and we've done everything else He's ever asked of us. I mean, after all, we'll be even more like Him so that has to be good, right?" God had given Adam and Eve the ability to reason and the freedom to choose. Just like we can't make someone authentically love and respect us, so God gave them the choice to love and respect Him. The liberty to choose Him and His Word over everything and enjoy perfect fellowship with God Himself was theirs.

The free will to reject God and His commands was also in their hearts; and now in their hands...in the form of a piece of fruit. But that choice comes in many forms for all of us. We all have rationalized and reasoned our way right into temptation. The moment we look away from the truths of God to focus on that which He forbids, we open our minds and hearts to deception, rationalization, compromise and spiritual death.

Rather than keep our focus on who God is, what His word demands of us and why we can and should trust His commands, we choose to focus on our own personal gain. Just like Adam and Eve, when we walk toward temptation, we walk away from truth. Once we lose sight of truth, and focus on temptation, we've lost our ability to resist. Selfishness consumes us, and while we think we're choosing something that will make our lives better, happier, easier, and more pleasurable, we are really choosing death.

They chose selfishly that day. They chose to think only of themselves. They chose to deny God's command and to seek after their own selfish gain. They were tricked into thinking they were choosing an even better life but in reality were choosing death. Spiritual death. Separation from God. The fall of man in the garden had nothing to do with what was in that fruit (good and evil). The fall was the result of their choice to disobey. Let me repeat that: the fall was a direct result of choosing to disobey the Word of God (Genesis 2:17). Whatever temptation you are holding in your hand, your heart, or your mind is the path to sin. Fruit isn't a sin, disobedience to God's boundaries is. Sex isn't a sin, disobedience to God's boundaries is. Food isn't a sin, disobedience to God's boundaries is. The Bible says when they ate the fruit (disobeyed God),

> *"the eyes of both of them were opened, and they knew that they were naked… and hid themselves from the presence of the Lord God."*
>
> *Genesis 3: 7–8*

Their innocence was gone. And as a result, they hid themselves from God. Sin changes us. It strips us of our purity and innocence and clothes us with death, guilt and shame. When we continue to embrace the sin as a lifestyle, our consciences are seared and our hearts become hard toward God and His word. At this point, many even take pride in their sinful lifestyle.

## A PILE OF ASHES

Mankind has been self-serving ever since that fateful day in Eden. Just like Adam and Eve, the moment we look toward temptation and away from God, our lust for power and more pleasure deceives us into thinking we are making a great choice to be our own bosses and to choose whatever feels good to us. Rather than obey God's loving commands to flee even the appearance of evil, we selfishly obey our own fleshly desires. We deceive ourselves into believing it's a life-giving choice. But just like Adam and Eve, we are deceived by the lust for more and in the end, we're left with spiritual death, guilt, and shame…a pile of ashes.

While sin is pleasurable for a season (Hebrews 11:24), Romans 6:23 also tells us that "the wages of sin is *death*". One of the principal powers each of us possess is our ability to choose. Consequently, every one of us has felt the sting of our poor choices and the poor choices of others. That sting of sin is the "death" that ensues; the death of our innocence and freedom. The death of our eternal communion and friendship with God, the Father. Because of Adam and Eve's selfish choice, they were defiled by sin.

Okay, so what? What's the big deal that Adam sinned? Because God is life. And God is holy and pure. Purity is just that—pure; undefiled; untainted; set apart. If God continued to be in fellowship, in oneness, with man, He would defile Himself. A holy God cannot have fellowship with that which is unholy or He would no longer be holy (or "*set apart*" from sin). The holy God, who is the embodiment of love, purity and selflessness would not and could not continue in intimate relationship with self-centered rebellion. Consequently, they lost their oneness with God, their Creator on that fateful day. Since then, man has continued attempting two things. One, to be their own god. Two, to reconnect with God either through Christ or through other false gods.

## UNCONDITIONAL LOVE

Even Adam and Eve's sin didn't change the fact that God loved them (and us) so deeply and unconditionally. Romans 8:39 tells us "…nothing can separate us from the love of God." I've seen just a glimpse of the love (and broken heart) of God in the eyes of godly parents who have lost their child to drug addiction. Their hearts are crushed. That child never dreamt that a little experimentation with a "harmless" recreational drug would put a hook in his nose and lead him into full blown bondage and addiction. Although that child knew the dangers, like Adam and Eve, he thought he was above the consequences. Oh, what his parents would give if they could bring their innocent child back to their loving arms, free from the grip of addiction!

I've seen God's unconditional love in the eyes of my dear friend who, though her husband left her and her small children for a life of homosexuality, never stopped loving him. Even after decades of hardship due to his choice to leave her and their children destitute, if he would have changed his ways, she would have taken him back because she loved him with such a pure love.

I can only picture that intense love and heartbreak in my parents' eyes when they sat holding me the day their baby girl was sent home from the hospital to die. Death was stealing their child from them.

What we would do in these circumstances, if only we had the power to change it and to make it all right again. Adam and Eve were powerless to undo the circumstances of their poor choice; just as we are powerless to undo all the devastation sin has wreaked in all of us since that first bite. As much as man would try, he is powerless against the grip of sin and death.

But God, the ultimate Abba Father, in His infinite love and power, did have the authority to do something about it. He could make a way to restore our life, purity and innocence and to restore the beautiful, pure, holy, intimate friendship He and mankind shared. He alone possesses the power to bring healing, peace, joy, and comfort where none can be found. But injustice demands justice. And justice demands retribution. God loved us so much, He was willing to take the punishment for our sins so that our relationship with Him could be restored! The blood of God's only Son became that retribution.

*"For God so loved the world,*
*that He gave His only begotten Son;*
*that whosoever believeth on Him,*
*shall not perish but have everlasting life."*
*John 3:16*

So why did Jesus, God's perfect son, choose to die in our place? Because He is love. Remember when He said, "I and the Father are one"? He knew the heart of Father God for Adam. It was His heart. For Adam. For Eve. For me. For you! And, unlike us, He had the power to restore our relationship to God the Father. Out of His love for the Father and the Father's love for us, He also made a choice: to lay down His life for others. To be the perfect, sacrificial lamb. Unlike Adam and Eve that fateful day in Eden, Jesus made the selfless choice to deny self and die in order to bring life to all who would also deny self (*choose death to self through obedience to Him*) and live for God. Jesus Christ made a way for us to truly live—to experience *abundant life!*

> *"The thief cometh not, but for to steal, and to kill, and to destroy:*
> **I am come that they might have life,**
> **and that they might have it more abundantly.**
> *I am the good Shepherd:*
> *the good Shepherd giveth His life for the sheep."*
>
> *John 10:10–11 (KJV)*

(Another version says it like this:)

> *"The thief's purpose is to steal and kill and destroy.*
> **My purpose is to give them a rich and satisfying life.**
> *"I am the good Shepherd.*
> *The good Shepherd sacrifices His life for the sheep."*
>
> *John 10:10–11 (NLT)*

> *"Christ redeemed us from the curse of the Law,*
> *having become a curse for us—for it is written,*
> *"CURSED IS EVERYONE WHO*
> *HANGS ON A TREE "*
>
> *Galatians 3:13 (AMP)*

## SO WHY THE CROSS?

Jesus died in the year 33 A.D. During that time, in that region, death by hanging on a cross was the death penalty for the worst offenders. If Jesus had chosen to come to earth in our day and age and lived in America, His death sentence would have been carried out through the electric chair as it is the most brutal penalty reserved for the worst offenders. That is what the cross represented in that time in history.

That should reveal to us a glimpse of the seriousness of sinning against God. He not only is our Creator, but no one and nothing has ever come close to loving us like He does or given us more than He has. Unlike everything else in all of creation, you and I are "fearfully and wonderfully made" by God in His image! He had the power and the right just to crush Adam and Eve like a bug for turning their backs on Him and rejecting Him that day, but He chose to love them and to cover their nakedness instead. His holiness demanded a penalty for sin. His *love* took that penalty upon Himself. And all who choose to be in right relationship to God, to them He gives eternal life.

*"And this is the way to have eternal life to know You,*
*the only true God, and Jesus Christ, the One You sent to earth."*

*John 17:3*

*"And this is the record, that God hath given to us eternal life,*
*and this life is in His Son."*

*1 John 5:11*

The first Adam, in the garden of Eden, brought spiritual death (eternal separation from God) and bondage *to* sin for all mankind by his selfish choice to "become like God". But Jesus, referred to in 1 Corinthians 15:45 as "the second Adam", in the garden of Gethsemane, brought freedom from sin and death to all mankind by His selfless choice to walk in perfect obedience to His heavenly Father. Apostle Paul put it this way:

*"While Jesus was here on earth, He offered prayers and pleadings,*
*with a loud cry and tears, to the One who could rescue Him*
*from death. And God heard His prayers*
*because of His deep reverence for God.*
*Even though Jesus was God's Son,*
*He learned obedience by the things which He suffered."*
*In this way, God qualified Him as a perfect High Priest,*

*and He became the source of eternal salvation*
*for all those who obey Him."*

*Hebrews 5:7–9 (NLT)*

Jesus *chose* to not only become fully man, and to suffer as a man (without sinning), but also to take God's wrath for sin upon Himself and to be offered up as the pure and perfect sacrifice for our guilt. The penalty for our sin was upon Him. He was the ransom paid to free us from being held captive by sin and death. He was the only one with the power to conquer death, hell, and the grave because, while He was fully human, He was without sin. He Himself became sin for us. I like how the amplified version of 2 Corinthians 5:21 says it:

*"He made Christ who knew no sin to [judicially] be sin on our behalf,*
*so that in Him we would become the righteousness of God*
*[that is, we would be made acceptable to Him and placed in a right relation-*
*ship with Him by His gracious lovingkindness]."*

## BEAUTY FOR ASHES

Christ never sinned. But God put our sin on Him that we could be made right with God because of what Christ has done for us! Christ's blood became the atonement, the legal transaction, of our sins for our salvation!

When you receive Christ into your heart to be who He is, the Lord and Savior of all mankind, then the blood that was poured out at Calvary's cross, becomes the atonement for your sin. His blood is the legal transaction that sets you free from the penalty of your sin (spiritual death and separation from God) and reunites you into intimate friendship and sonship with God the Father! You are brought from spiritual death to life. Your debt is wiped clean. You're given a new beginning, a new life!

*"Therefore if anyone is in Christ, he is a new creature;*
*the old things passed away; behold, new things have come.*

*Now all these things are from God, who reconciled us to Himself*
*through Christ and gave us the ministry of reconciliation, namely,*
*that God was in Christ reconciling the world to Himself,*
*not counting their trespasses against them,*
*and He has committed to us the word of reconciliation.*
*He made Him who knew no sin to be sin on our behalf,*
*so that we might become the righteousness of God in Him."*
*2 Corinthians 5:17–19, 21 (NASB)*

Where we were once slaves to sin, belonging to the evil one, we are now sons (and daughters) of God, free from the bondage of sin. John put it this way:

*"Jesus answered them, Verily, verily, I say unto you,*
*Whosoever committeth sin is the servant of sin.*
*And the servant abideth not in the house for ever:*
*but the Son abideth ever.*
*If the Son therefore shall make you free,*
*ye shall be free indeed."*
*John 8:34–36 (KJV)*

When we invite Jesus Christ into our hearts to be the ruler of our lives, we are set free from the power of sin that separates us from God and we then become "joint-heirs with Christ". Because our position as a child of God is restored, the Bible says we receive all the fringe benefits of sonship:

*"Therefore, dear brothers and sisters, you have no obligation to do*
*what your sinful nature urges you to do. For if you live by its dictates,*
*you will die. But if through the power of the Spirit [of God]*
*you put to death the deeds of your sinful nature, you will live.*
*For all who are led by the Spirit of God are children of God.*
*So you have not received a spirit that makes you fearful slaves.*
*Instead, you received God's Spirit when He adopted you*

*as His own children. Now we call Him, "Abba, Father."*
*For His Spirit joins with our spirit to affirm that we are God's children.*
**And since we are His children, we are His heirs.**
**In fact, together with Christ we are heirs of God's**
**glory . . . "**

*Romans 8:12–17 (NLT)*

## THE ULTIMATE RELATIONSHIP

I can't emphasize this enough: the greatest *miracle* you will ever experience is your salvation found in Christ. It is the greatest miracle of my life! Being able to have an intimate friendship with God has been my most valued treasure in life. He has been my closest friend for 50 years now. It's been the one constant in my life that only gets better with the passing years.

He truly is " . . . a friend that sticks closer than a brother" (Proverbs 18:24). He knows every fault I have, every sin I've ever committed, and has always extended His love, forgiveness, and healing every time I've come to Him with a repentant heart. His compassions fail not, His mercies are new every morning (Lamentations 3:22–23), His strength is made perfect in my weakness, and His grace is sufficient for anything I ever face. (2 Corinthians 12:19).

## HIS WORD AND HIS SPIRIT ARE ALIVE AND AT WORK

Yes, I talk to God and He talks to me. That's called prayer. Prayer is not a one-way conversation. It's communion; fellowship with God. I cannot say He's ever spoken to me in an audible voice. I can say, however, He has spoken so strongly to my heart at times it has almost seemed like an audible voice.

One example of how God will speak to us is what just happened in the last 24 hours of writing this. I went to church last night. During the service, I was so troubled in my spirit by what I was feeling. I can't tell you when I've ever walked out of a good church service, but last night I had to get out of there. I was so overwhelmed by what I was feeling, I could hardly breathe. My chest was so tight, I felt as if I was going to have a heart attack. I drove straight to a godly friend's house and poured my heart out to her and her husband. As I wept and shared my broken, burdened heart with them, she told me (after the fact) that she was silently praying for the Holy Spirit to make it clear to her what she should say to me. As the Holy Spirit lead her, she told me what she saw and felt in her heart that God was calling me to do. She had no way of knowing the specific things she was speaking of nor that it was a total confirmation of what was in my heart but had shared with no one. It was a calling that was so out-of-the-box and scary to me.

The next morning, while in prayer, I cried out to God, "Lord, that calling and vision is so much bigger than I am. Honestly, it scares me to death! It will quite literally, require the power of God for me to do what you're calling me to because there is no way I can do this. This is one time I need a really big confirmation to step into this call. I can't afford to misunderstand you on this. I need very clear confirmation from more than one source." I went on to pray and to worship Him for another hour or so and then sat down to write some more of this book. While writing, another very godly friend texted me. She had been sitting next to me in the service last night and had texted me this morning to make sure I was okay since I left the service early. I had told her that I was fine but just left because I wasn't feeling well and I left out all the details and the fact I felt like I was about to have a heart attack. She just texted me a thumbs up and that was the end of that conversation this morning. But while sitting here, this afternoon, working on my book, I received another text from her immediately followed by several long texts that completely blew my mind.

She proceeded to tell me that, while she was singing and worshipping during the congregational songs, she felt like maybe the Lord was showing her something concerning Jonathan and me and a "calling" she saw on our lives. She briefly described it and then asked if that bears witness with me. It was dead-on! She had no way of knowing it was what God had put in my heart and what my other friend had shared with me the night before! When I texted her back and told her that it absolutely bore witness with me, she sent me several more texts describing in detail what the Lord had shown her concerning us. What she said in the texts was so remarkably detailed and accurate. It went right along with the scripture God had given me two days earlier while I was alone in prayer (and had told no one), what He had spoken to my other friend the night before, and what He was showing me in my prayer time this morning! These two friends of mine do not know each other. And furthermore, I never sit with this lady in church. We just happened to be at the service without our husbands and randomly bumped into each other.

God will speak to us in any number of ways—He's not limited to any one way. However, whatever He speaks to us, always lines up with His written Word (the Bible). He speaks to us mainly through His written Word, by the leading of His Holy Spirit. The reason the Bible tells us in Psalm 119:11 "Thy Word have I hid in my heart that I might not sin against God" is because the Bible is the Word of God. It's His heart expressing His love for us. It's His instruction book for our lives filled with all the wisdom, knowledge, insight, and power we need to overcome in life. The more we memorize scripture (hide it in our heart), the more He can bring the right Scripture at the right moment to our mind to lead us and to protect us. You may be thinking, "Ummm...hello?! There's no way I could memorize the whole Bible!" I don't mean literally memorize the whole Bible but key passages of scripture that jump off the page and resonate with your spirit when you are reading and studying it. The more you read the Bible, the more it becomes embedded in your heart and mind. Remember, the Bible is not just a book. It's the *living* Word of God.

*"For the word of God is living and active and full of power [making it operative, energizing, and effective]. It is sharper than any two-edged sword,*

*penetrating as far as the division of the soul and spirit [the completeness of*
*a person], and of both joints and marrow [the deepest parts of our nature],*
*exposing and judging the very thoughts and intentions of the heart."*

*Hebrews 4:12 (AMP)*

*"In the beginning was the Word.*
*And the Word was with God and the Word was God.*
*The same was in the beginning with God.*
*All things were made by Him;*
*and without Him was not anything made that was made.*
*In Him was life; and the life was the light of men.*
*The light shineth in the darkness,*
*and the darkness comprehended it not...*
*That was the true Light,*
*which lighteth every man that cometh into the world.*
*He was in the world, and the world was made by Him,*
*and the world knew Him not.*
*But as many as received Him,*
*to them gave He power to become the sons of God,*
*even to them that believe on His name:*
*Which were born, not of blood, nor of the will of the flesh,*
*nor of the will of man, but of God.*
*And the Word was made flesh, and dwelt among us,*
*(and we beheld His glory,*
*the glory as of the only begotten of the Father,)*
*full of grace and truth."*

*John 1:1–10,12–14 (KJV)*

When we have accepted Jesus Christ into our hearts as Lord and
Savior, His spirit enables us to understand and to retain the truth of
Scripture as we read and study it. It literally possesses the power to
completely transform your life!

*"Do not conform to the pattern of this world,*
*but be transformed by the renewing of your mind.*

*Then you will be able to test and approve what God's will is—*
*His good, pleasing and perfect will."*
Romans 12:2(NIV)

Your mind is quite literally transformed and renewed by reading and studying the Bible, God's Word.

*"So then faith cometh by hearing, and hearing*
*by the Word of God."*
Romans 10:17

Ninety-nine percent of the Scriptures in this book have come to my mind as I'm writing. I don't need to go hunting through the Bible to find Scriptures to support what I'm saying because I have them in my mind and heart. Now I may not know the entire passage or remember the exact location (Scripture reference), but I have enough of it memorized that I can quickly look it up in a Bible concordance or google it for the reference (by 'reference' I mean which book, chapter and verse in the Bible). Now don't beat yourself up if you don't know scripture. We all have to start at the beginning. Remember, I've been reading the Bible since I was was "knee high to a grasshopper" and I'm over 50 years of age. I *should* have a lot memorized by now! And because of that, I can personally testify to you that it truly has the power to change your life. It even has the power to heal your physical body, as well as your mind and spirit. That is precisely how I conquered cancer, chemo, addiction, hypothyroidism and so much more. When we "live, and move, and have our being" in Christ and His Holy Word, He will speak to us, heal us, empower us, and do exceedingly, abundantly more than we could ask or think in us and through us! I can't emphasize it enough: start memorizing Scripture. And keep on memorizing Scripture until the day you graduate to heaven.

*"I can do all things through Christ who gives me strength."*
Philippians 4:13 (NIV)

## PRAYER

"Jesus, I thank you for the incomprehensible price you paid at the cross for me. I thank you for laying down Your kingly crown of glory to wear a thorn of crowns that represented my sin. Yes, LORD, my sin became Your crown so that I could receive the crown of life! You died so I can have (spiritual) life. You were beaten beyond recognition so I could be healed and whole. Forgive me, for I have sinned against You and You alone [confess your sins right now as they come to mind, asking God for forgiveness]. Please, Jesus, come into my heart and take over. I surrender my heart and life to you and make You Lord (boss) of me. Thank you for taking my guilt, sin, and shame and clothing me in Your robe of righteousness. I am now a child of the most high God; joint-heirs with Christ (Romans 8:17). The power that raised Christ from the dead now dwells within me and empowers me to live a pure life, in a personal relationship with You, my God. Thank You! Thank You! Thank You! Amen!"

## FOR REFLECTION AND APPLICATION

### MEMORIZE John 3:16:

*"For God so loved the world that He gave His only begotten son. That whosoever believeth in Him shall not perish, but have everlasting life."*

### MEMORIZE 2 Corinthians 5:17:

*"Therefore if any man be in Christ, he is a new creature: old things are passed away; behold, all things are become new."*

### MEDITATE on these scriptures

*John 3, Romans 8:17, 1 Corinthians 1:20, 2 Corinthians 5:17, Isaiah 61:10 & Colossians 2:9–17.*

*Write down what these verses mean to you.*

### MANDATE

*Tell someone today what Jesus has done for you. If you have never been baptized in water, make that commitment today.*

# *Notes*

*Chapter Four*

# WHAT'S KEEPING YOU FROM YOUR MIRACLE?

*"Ask and it will be given to you; seek and you will find;*
*knock and the door will be opened to you."*
*Matthew 7:7 (NIV)*

GOD LOVES YOU more than you can comprehend and He has a purpose for your life. The greatest miracle mankind can ever experience in this life is a personal relationship with their Creator. But how is it possible for me or you, or anyone for that matter, to honestly have a close friendship with the God of the universe? That seems ridiculously unattainable, right? But what's impossible with man, is possible with God! After all, He has all power. He is all powerful. He can do whatever He chooses because He is, well, GOD! Based on personal experience, I can assure you it is possible for you to have this kind of relationship. Just the fact that you are reading this book means that the Spirit of God is calling you to Himself. You may think it's chance, curiosity, desperation, or even obligation; but God has ordained this moment in your life to draw you closer to Him. He wants to have a personal relationship with you. And not just any relationship, but the closest, most profound relationship you could possibly experience. It's a relationship that will radically change everything in your life, for all eternity. The following passages make this implicitly clear:

> *"For God so loved the world*
> *that He gave His only begotten son,*
> *that whosoever believeth on Him would not perish*
> *but have everlasting life."*
>
> *John 3:16 (KJV)*

> *Jesus said, "I am come that they might have life*
> *and that they might have it more abundantly'."*
>
> *John 10:10(KJV)*

## THE BAD NEWS

Our sin has separated us from God and holds us hostage, preventing us from the freedom of entering into that beautiful relationship with God. All of us have committed sin. Sin against our own bodies. Sin against others. Sin against our Creator and holy God; living to gratify the lusts of the flesh and not the Spirit of God. The consequence of sin is spiritual death; eternal separation from God. So what exactly is sin? And what are the full ramifications of it? This is what the Bible says about it:

> *"Don't you realize that those who do wrong*
> *will not inherit the Kingdom of God?*
> ***Don't fool yourselves.***
> *Those who indulge in sexual sin,*
> *or who worship idols, or commit adultery,*
> *or are male prostitutes, or practice homosexuality,*
> *or are thieves, or greedy people, or drunkards,*
> *or are abusive, or cheat people*
> *none of these will inherit the Kingdom of God."*
>
> *1 Corinthians 6:9–10 (NLT)*

*"So I say, **let the Holy Spirit guide your lives.***
***Then you won't be doing what your sinful nature craves.***
*The sinful nature wants to do evil,*
*which is just the opposite of what the Spirit wants.*
*And the Spirit gives us desires that are the opposite*
*of what the sinful nature desires.*
*These two forces are constantly fighting each other,*
*so you are not free to carry out your good intentions…*
*When you follow the desires of your sinful nature,*
*the results are very clear:*
*sexual immorality, impurity, lustful pleasures,*
*idolatry, sorcery, hostility, quarreling, jealousy,*
*outbursts of anger, selfish ambition, dissension,*
*division, envy, drunkenness, wild parties,*
*and other sins like these.*
*Let me tell you again, as I have before,*
*that anyone living that sort of life*
*will not inherit the Kingdom of God."*

*Galatians 5:16–17, 19–21 (NLT)*

*"But cowards, unbelievers, the corrupt, murderers,*
*the immoral, those who practice witchcraft,*
*idol worshipers, and all liars—their fate is in*
*the fiery lake of burning sulfur.*
*This is the second death."*

*Revelation 21:8 (NLT)*

God is pure and holy (set apart). He cannot have union (fellowship, communion, intimate friendship) with that which is unholy (impure) or else He Himself would not be holy (pure; undefiled). The Bible puts it this way:

*"All have sinned and fall short of the glory of God"*

*Romans 3:23*

*"The result of sin is death…" (separation from God)*

*Romans 6:23a*

## THE GOOD NEWS

It is only through Jesus Christ that freedom from our debt of sin is paid and we are redeemed from the curse of death and hell. No one has to die in their sin and go to hell. No one. The way has been provided. The cross of Jesus Christ bridged the gap between us and God. When you give your life to Jesus you become spiritually "born again". Being born again is a spiritual work of the Holy Spirit in you:

*"Jesus replied, 'I tell you the truth,*
*unless you are born again,*
*you cannot see the Kingdom of God….*
*I assure you,*
*no one can enter the Kingdom of God*
*without being born of water and the Spirit.*
*Humans can reproduce only human life,*
*but the Holy Spirit gives birth to spiritual life.*
*So don't be surprised when I say,*
*"You must be born again".*
*The wind blows wherever it wants.*
*Just as you can hear the wind but can't tell*
*where it comes from or where it is going,*
*so you can't explain how people are born of the Spirit.'"*

*John 3:3, 5–8 (NLT)*

When we receive Jesus Christ as our Lord and Savior, our old, spiritually dead life is over. The eyes of our understanding are opened and we are born again. The Bible says:

*"….anyone who belongs to Christ has become a new person.*
*The old life is gone; a new life has begun!*

*And all of this is a gift from God,*
*who brought us back to Himself through Christ…*
*For God was in Christ, reconciling the world to Himself,*
*no longer counting people's sins against them.*
*And He gave us this wonderful message of reconciliation.*
*So we are Christ's ambassadors;*
*God is making His appeal through us.*
*We speak for Christ when we plead, 'Come back to God!'*
**For God made Christ, who never sinned,**
**to be the offering for our sin,**
**so that we could be made right with God**
**through Christ."**

*2 Corinthians 5:17–21 (NLT)*

*"For the result of sin is death but the gift of God is eternal life*
*through Jesus Christ our Lord."*

*Romans 6:23 (KJV)*

*"God demonstrates His own love toward us in this:*
*While we were still sinners, Christ died for us"*

*Romans 5:8 (NIV)*

God knows that we are helpless in our sin. So He did for us what we cannot do for ourselves. God sent His Son to die as a penalty for our sins. But it didn't end with His death on the cross. He rose again and still lives! Jesus died in our place so that we could have a personal relationship with Him *now* and live with Him in all eternity!

## WOULD YOU LIKE TO RECEIVE GOD'S FORGIVENESS?

We can't earn salvation. We are saved by God's grace when we have faith in His Son, Jesus Christ. Christianity is the only religion in the world that is based on God's work on the cross not our own works, lest any man should boast. Every other religion requires us working our way to a god who will determine if we are good enough, based on our works, to enter into a better afterlife. However, the one true God knew we could never attain being good enough to be pure and holy as He is pure and holy. So, out of His pure, unconditional love for us, He paid the price for our redemption. All you have to do is realize and confess that you are a sinner, that Jesus Christ died for your sins, and ask Him for His forgiveness. Then turn from your sins—that's called repentance—and give Him lordship of your heart and life. Jesus Christ knows you and loves you. What matters to Him is the attitude of your heart; your honesty. If you have never given your heart and life to Jesus Christ and made Him the Lord (master) of your life and would like to do that, then pray the following prayer from your heart. I encourage you to get down on your knees, if possible, and bow humbly before God when you speak this prayer. As you pray, truly believe in your heart that Jesus is the Son of God and you will be saved and made new in Him:

*"Dear Lord Jesus, I know that I am a sinner, and I ask for Your forgiveness. I believe You are the Son of the Living God and died to pay the penalty for my sins and then rose from the dead. I trust and follow You as my Lord and Savior. I lay down my life, my agenda, and choose to follow You and obey You. Please come live in my heart and change me from the inside out. Guide my life and empower me to do Your will as I give You the lead and I follow. In Your name I pray. Amen."*

Congratulations! If you prayed that prayer with all sincerity of heart, you are now a child of God, "joint heirs with Christ" (Romans 8:17)! Born again. That now means every promise in the Bible is yours (2 Corinthians 1:20); His Holy Spirit has come into your life and God is now your Heavenly Father! You have passed from (spiritual) death to life! God is for you, not against you. He no longer holds your sin debt against you—it's been wiped clean by the atoning blood of Jesus!

*"The faithful love of the LORD never ends!*
*His mercies never cease.*
*Great is His faithfulness;*
*His mercies begin afresh each morning."*
*Lamentations 3:22–23*

*"…Jesus prayed this prayer:*
*'O Father, Lord of heaven and earth,*
*thank you for hiding these things from*
*those who think themselves wise and clever,*
*and for revealing them to the childlike.*
*Yes, Father, it pleased You to do it this way!*
*My Father has entrusted everything to me.*
*No one truly knows the Son except the Father,*
*and no one truly knows the Father except the Son*
*and those to whom the Son chooses to reveal Him.'*
*Then Jesus said,*
**'Come to Me, all of you who are weary**
**and carry heavy burdens, and I will give you rest.**
*Take My yoke upon you. Let Me teach you,*
*because I am humble and gentle at heart,*
*and you will find rest for your souls.*
*For My yoke is easy to bear,*
*and the burden I give you is light.'"*
*Matthew 11:25–30 (NLT)*

*Jesus praying to God, the Father, said:*
*"And I give Myself as a holy sacrifice for them*
*so they can be made holy by Your truth...*
*I pray that they will all be one,*
*just as You and I are one—*
*as You are in Me, Father, and I am in You.*
*And may they be in Us*
*so that the world will believe You sent Me.*

*"I have given them the glory You gave Me,*
*so they may be one as We are One.*
*I am in them and You are in Me.*
*May they experience such perfect unity*
*that the world will know that you sent me*
*and that You love them as much as You love Me."*

*John 17:19, 21–23 (NLT)*

## THE GREATEST MIRACLE OF YOUR LIFE

Salvation is the greatest miracle gift anyone could receive. If a personal relationship with God is the the only miracle He ever does in our lives, it would certainly be more than enough for each of us to live a life of blissful gratitude! But we have a God who desires to bless us above and beyond what we could ever ask or think (Eph.3:20). He is a God who desires to "crown our years with bountiful harvests and cause even the hard pathways in our lives to overflow with abundance" (Psalm 65:11). When the disciples were excited because they could perform miracles (casting out demons), Jesus put it all in perfect perspective:

*"And [they] returned again with joy, saying, Lord, even the devils are subject unto us through Thy name. And He [Jesus] said unto them, 'I beheld Satan as lightning fall from heaven. Behold, I give unto you power to tread on serpents and scorpions, and over all the power of the enemy: and nothing shall by any means hurt you. Notwithstanding in this, rejoice not, that the spirits are subject unto you; but rather rejoice, because your names are written in heaven.'"*

*Luke 10:17–20 (KJV)*

The outward manifestation (or "fruit") of being born again is explained in Galatians:

*"But the Holy Spirit produces this kind of fruit in our lives:*
*love, joy, peace, patience, kindness, goodness,*

*faithfulness, gentleness, and self-control.*
*There is no law against these things!*
*Those who belong to Christ Jesus have nailed*
*the passions and desires of their sinful nature*
*to His cross and crucified them there.*
*Since we are living by the Spirit,*
*let us follow the Spirit's leading in every part of our lives."*
*Galatians 5:22–25 (NLT)*

The more time you spend loving Him by reading and studying the Bible, memorizing key passages, praying, worshipping and singing praise songs from your heart to Him, the more the Holy Spirit will work in your life, transforming you into a new person. Jesus also made it clear that we are to tell others what He has done in our lives and to love and to serve others in His name. If you're asking yourself, "Where do I begin? How then do I live this out?" start with this main passage of scripture from the Gospel of Matthew:

*"Jesus replied, 'You must love the LORD your God*
*with all your heart, all your soul, and all your mind.*
*This is the first and greatest commandment.*
*A second is equally important:*
*Love your neighbor as yourself.*
*The entire law and all the demands of the prophets*
*are based on these two commandments.'"*
*Matthew 22:37–40 (NLT)*

I can't emphasize enough how vital it is, for every area of your life, to build your faith by delving into the Bible; reading and studying it (starting with the New Testament). Begin memorizing key verses to begin building a solid foundation for your life. (See chapter 7 for key passages for memorization.)

The Bible, the Word of God, is the most powerful tool in your arsenal for learning who God is, how much He loves you, and the plan and purpose He has for your life.

*"So then faith cometh by hearing,*
*and hearing by the word of God."*

*Romans 10:17 (KJV)*

*"If Your instructions hadn't sustained me with joy,*
*I would have died in my misery.*
*I will never forget Your commandments,*
*for by them You give me life...*
*Oh, how I love Your instructions!*
*I think about them all day long.*
*Your commands make me wiser than my enemies,*
*for they are my constant guide.*
*Yes, I have more insight than my teachers,*
*for I am always thinking of Your laws.*
*I am even wiser than my elders,*
*for I have kept Your commandments.*
*I have refused to walk on any evil path,*
*so that I may remain obedient to Your word...*
*Your commandments give me understanding;*
*no wonder I hate every false way of life.*
*Your word is a lamp to guide my feet and a light for my path...*
*I have suffered much, O LORD;*
*restore my life again as you promised.*
*LORD, accept my offering of praise,*
*and teach me Your regulations...*
*Your laws are my treasure; they are my heart's delight.*
*I am determined to keep Your decrees to the very end...*
*You are my refuge and my shield;*
*Your word is my source of hope."*

*Psalms 119:92–93, 97–101,104–105,*
*107–108, 111–112, 114 (NLT)*

In the Old Testament times as well as the New Testament times, those who accomplished great things for God were first anointed by the Holy Spirit, and endued with power from on high. No great work has ever been accomplished except through the power of the Holy Spirit. The Holy Spirit is the Great Executive of God, carrying out the will of God in and through His people. He exists to carry out the commands of God. The very first record of the existence and operation of the Holy Spirit starts in Genesis 1:2; "*... the Spirit of God moved on the face of the waters.*" Job understood that it was through the power of the Spirit of God all things were created, when he said in Job 26:13, *"By His Spirit He hath garnished the heavens.."* Even Job's friend understood it when he said, in chapter 33:4, *"The Spirit of God hath made me..."*. It was the Holy Spirit who came upon Mary enabling her to conceive the Messiah. When the angel of the Lord told Mary she would conceive and bring forth the Son of God, Mary said, "How can this be, since I am a virgin?" The Angel answered and said to her, *"The Holy Spirit will come upon you and the power of the Highest will overshadow you; therefore, also, that Holy One that is born will be called the Son of God"* (Luke 1:31–35). The Holy Spirit is the source of all life. John 6:63 says, *"It is the Spirit that quickeneth,"* or giveth life so that in God *"we live and move and have our being" (Acts 17:28).*

Scientists have sought in vain to discover the source of life, never realizing that the Spirit of God is the great source of all life. In Acts 2, on the Day of Pentecost, the disciples were all together, "in one accord". *"And suddenly"*, verse 2 tells us, *"there came a sound from heaven, as if a rushing mighty wind, and it filled the whole house where they were sitting. Then there appeared to them divided tongues, as of fire, and one sat upon each of them, and they were all filled with the Holy Spirit and began to speak with other tongues, as the Spirit gave them utterance."*

> *"And when they came to the disciples, they saw a great crowd around them, and scribes arguing with them. And immediately all the crowd, when they saw Him, were greatly amazed and ran up to Him and greeted Him. And He asked them, 'What are you arguing about with them?' And someone from the crowd answered Him, 'Teacher, I brought*

*my son to You, for he has a spirit that makes him mute. And whenever it seizes him, it throws him down, and he foams and grinds his teeth and becomes rigid. So I asked Your disciples to cast it out, and they were not able.' And He answered them, 'O faithless generation, how long am I to be with you? How long am I to bear with you? Bring him to Me.' And they brought the boy to Him. And when the spirit saw Him, immediately it convulsed the boy, and he fell on the ground and rolled about, foaming at the mouth. And Jesus asked his father, 'How long has this been happening to him?' And he said, 'From childhood. And it has often cast him into fire and into water, to destroy him. But if You can do anything, have compassion on us and help us.' And Jesus said to him, 'If You can?* **All things are possible for one who believes.'** *Immediately the father of the child cried out and said, 'I believe; help my unbelief!' And when Jesus saw that a crowd came running together, He rebuked the unclean spirit, saying to it, 'You mute and deaf spirit, I command you, come out of him and never enter him again.' And after crying out and convulsing him terribly, it came out, and the boy was like a corpse, so that most of them said, 'He is dead.' But Jesus took him by the hand and lifted him up, and he arose. And when He had entered the house, His disciples asked Him privately, 'Why could we not cast it out?' And He said to them, 'This kind cannot be driven out by anything but prayer and fasting.'"*

*Mark 9:14–29 (ESV)*

## WHAT INHIBITS THE MIRACULOUS FLOW IN OUR LIVES?

According to scripture, there are several things that can stop the flow of the miraculous into our lives. Fortunately, when we honestly accept the Truth, and walk in it, we can remove the hindrances and release the supernatural into our lives: mind, spirit and body! Though it's usually spoken 'body, mind and spirit', when mentioning the three together, I put them in the order of *'mind, spirit, body'* for a reason. Proverbs states:

*"For as he thinketh in his heart, so is he..."*
*Proverbs 27:3 (KJV)*

We must first hear the truth about God's Word to know what is available to us. But even though we may hear, know it and even memorize it, at the end of the day, what does the mind of your heart say? Just because you say with your mouth that you believe, your mind (heart) can believe the opposite. Scripture puts it like this:

*"But let him ask in faith, nothing wavering.*
*For he that wavereth is like a wave of the sea*
*driven with the wind and tossed.*
*For let not that man think*
*that he shall receive any thing of the Lord.*
*A double-minded man is unstable in all his ways."*
*James 1:6–8 (KJV)*

## WHERE ARE THE MIRACLES?

Churches are filled with people who *say* they *believe* in miracles. So why aren't we *seeing* them in the church on a regular basis? I'm talking about the *"big"* miracles. The kind that shout loudly to unbelievers, "This Jesus-stuff is real!" Could it be that we don't really understand what the Bible says about miracles? Could it be that we know what it says, but we just don't really believe it's for us? Or, could it be that we know what it says, we believe it, but aren't willing to do what's required to *walk* in it? When we choose to be intellectually honest with ourselves and take a good look at our belief system (not what we say we believe but what we really, in our hearts, believe and our actions validate) then we can move forward.

*"So Jesus said to the Jews who had believed Him,*
*'If you abide in My word, you are truly My disciples,*
*and you will know the Truth, and the Truth will set you free.'"*
*John 8:31–32 ESV*

Jesus was encouraging them to abide in His teaching, rely on His promises, and obey His commands. The power of Jesus' statement lies in the deep waters of the word *"abide"*.

To *abide* means:

- to **remain**; **continue**; **stay**.
- to **dwell; reside.**
- to **continue in** a particular condition, attitude, **relationship**, etc.
- **to stand in; to endure, sustain, or withstand without yielding or submitting** (to anything else).
- **to abide a vigorous onslaught.**
- **to wait for**; await.
- **to accept without opposition or question.**
- **to pay the price or penalty of; suffer for.**
- **to act in accord with.**
- to **submit to**; **agree to.**
- **to remain steadfast or faithful to**; keep.

Wow! **Abide**. Therein lies the power of the supernatural becoming a consistent part of our lives. It's not enough to just hear His Word, we must *live* in it. Those definitions denote living, moving, and having our being in them (Acts 17:28). **It is dwelling upon and believing in them so strongly that it becomes central to everything we are**; so much so that ***nothing*** can move us from that position.

- Not fear.
- Not fiery trials and suffering.
- Not sickness.
- Not disappointments or setbacks.
- Not opposition or vigorous onslaught.
- Not death.
- ***NOTHING.***

It is choosing to let His presence and His truths become so integrated in every part of our lives that the result is the possession of an unshakable confidence in Him that the world (and most religious people) can't comprehend; a peace and confidence that goes beyond man's ability to understand. Jesus isn't talking here about abiding in a church group or a denomination or religion. You can be the most faithful member of the local Catholic, Baptist, Pentecostal, Methodist, Presbyterian, or any other church in town. You might even be the Priest, Pastor, Bishop or Elder. **None of these positions mean anything if you're not abiding in Christ *and* His living Word** (the two are one and go hand-in-hand in true communion with Christ).

Before you continue reading, go back and read that Scripture again along with the definitions of "abide". Take a few minutes, or more, to marinate in it. Let those words really sink into the "mind" of your heart and the "heart" of your mind. Within that truth lies the key to unlocking the mysterious and great power of God and releasing it into your everyday life. Jesus further explains the meaning of "abiding" in Him in chapter 15 with the illustration of the vine:

> *"I am the true vine, and My Father is the vinedresser.*
> *Every branch in Me that does not bear fruit He takes away,*
> *and every branch that does bear fruit He prunes,*
> *that it may bear more fruit."*
>
> *John 15:2*

That verse is a great word picture to illustrate that if we are true followers of Christ and truly abiding in Him, we are expected to bear fruit (or to present evidence) of the power of Christ living in us. If we're not bearing fruit, we are pruned to bear fruit, just like a vine is pruned after harvest so that it will bear more the following year. He explains it further as He continues speaking:

> ***"Abide in Me, and I in you.***
> *As the branch cannot bear fruit by itself,*

*unless it **abides** in the vine, neither can you,*
*unless you abide in Me.*
*I am the vine; you are the branches.*
*Whoever **abides** in Me and I in him,*
*he it is that bears much fruit,*
*for apart from Me you can do nothing.*
*If anyone does not **abide** in Me*
*he is thrown away like a branch and withers;*
*and the branches are gathered, thrown into the fire, and burned.*
***If you abide in Me, and My words abide in you,***
***ask whatever you wish, and it will be done for you.***
***By this My Father is glorified,***
***that you bear much fruit and so prove to be My***
***disciples…..***
*As the Father has loved Me, so have I loved you.*
***Abide** in My love.*
*If you keep My commandments, you will **abide** in My love,*
*just as I have kept My Father's commandments*
*and **abide** in His love.*
*These things I have spoken to you,*
***that My joy may be in you,***
***and that your joy may be full."***
*John 15:1–2, 4–11 (ESV)*

## PEEL AWAY THE FACADE OF RELIGION

To unveil the reality of why you are not experiencing the divine supernatural at work in your life, you must be willing to peel away the facade of religion and delve into the realms of your true belief system. I hear "believers" contradict themselves all the time. They will say they believe that God is their Healer and then turn right around and contradict it with their words and actions.

A couple weeks ago, at a church luncheon, an elderly woman fell and skinned her knee and elbow in the auditorium. Several of us helped her up into a chair and then prayed for God to touch her and heal her from any possible injuries as a result of the fall. As soon as we finished praying one of the ladies immediately declared, "Boy are you going to be hurting tomorrow!" I thought to myself,*'Based on that confession, you don't even believe what you just prayed!'* Unfortunately, that happens a lot.

I remember in college, travelling with a singing group that I was a part of. We were ministering at a church out of state and were there for the weekend. During our day off, we all went to a hosting family's ranch to ride four-wheelers. Rhoda, one of the girls from our group was riding on the back of one of the four-wheelers, while Brian, one of the guys in our group, was driving (sitting like two people on a motorcycle). As Rhoda recalls, "We were having a great time! Brian was driving fast, and I was laughing and enjoying the ride. Suddenly, Brian hits a bump. I flew up from the seat and came back down, slamming my backside on the steel bar behind the seat. When I hit the seat, I heard a cracking sound, and felt excruciating pain in the area of my tailbone. I cried out for Brian to stop. When we came to a halt, I literally slithered off the four-wheeler onto the ground."

She was unable to get up or to even move due to the excruciating pain in her back. We prayed, in that moment, for God to completely heal her. That is when the miracle happened. Within seconds of the prayer, I reached my hand out for her. She took my hand and was able to easily stand up and walk around without pain or numbness. As she walked, she was saying, "Oh my! Oh my!" Everyone was amazed! I never forgot that day and have pondered it many times since. Our ensemble sang that evening and she stood (in heels) for over an hour with no pain whatsoever! After reminiscing with her a couple months ago, she told me, "I have had zero back pain to this day—and I am 50!"

Our true belief system is found not only in the confession of our mouth but in the manifestations thereof. What do our actions say? What is our reaction when faced with a problem bigger than our ability to solve? What is our reaction to the hard truths of the Scriptures? What is holding you back from 'stepping out of the boat' to walk by faith and not by sight? What is keeping you from believing to the point of giving up your own agenda, desires, pride, and comfort to embrace the promises of God no matter what it costs you? Is it fear? Is it hurt from the past? Do you really believe a relationship with Jesus is worth all that? Or Is it that you just can't begin to grasp how much God loves you and wants to bless you with true freedom found in a deep intimate friendship with Him when you surrender your life to Him? Many Christians are not even willing to fast and pray for a day or more just to draw closer to the Lord. And sadly, most are not willing to give up TV or secular music and media to 'come out of the camp' and seek after God with all their minds, hearts, and strength. Many call themselves Christians yet are completely unwilling to confess and repent of their sin. And many are held captive by unforgiveness.

## UNFORGIVENESS: A DEATH SENTENCE

Unforgiveness is so contrary to everything Jesus lived and taught. While we know His crucifixion was the ultimate expression of love and forgiveness, His life was also a continual example of forgiving others. When reading the Gospels (the first four chapters of the New Testament), we see how Jesus lived a lifestyle of forgiveness. He faced resistance, rejection, and betrayal from family, close friends, disciples, and religious "experts". Yet Jesus never held a grudge or let any of their actions deter or distract Him from His life's purpose. He remained free from bitterness and unforgiveness at every turn. Though He was God, He was still fully human and had the free will to give place to anger and resentment and to allow it to take root in His heart. The key to His victory over these temptations was in His oneness with God, His Father (John 5:30). We must abide daily in spiritual oneness with the Holy Spirit who strengthens us to do all things through Christ in us. That is why He sent His Holy Spirit;

to empower us to be like Him. We can and must forgive those who have trespassed against us. No matter how deep the hurt and offense, the Holy Spirit will do the healing in you if you are willing to surrender your hurt, anger, and unforgiveness to Him.

> *"And when you stand praying,*
> *if you hold anything against anyone, forgive them,*
> *so that your Father in heaven*
> *may forgive you your sins."*
> Mark 11:25–26

When (my husband) Jonathan and I were pastoring in the Napa Valley, we had an elderly lady that attended the church. Betty (not her real name) was "a strong Christian" in most people's eyes. She taught a children's Sunday School class, was always willing to volunteer and was at church most every time the doors were open.

Years before we knew her, Betty had experienced tremendous pain and tragedy in her life. One day, she and her husband, along with her two small boys, were enjoying a day of boating on the lake. Since she had never learned to swim, she sat in the boat as her husband and two boys jumped in the water for a swim. To her horror, she watched helplessly as an undertow ferociously jerked her husband and two little boys under water. Her husband's strength was no match for the power of that undercurrent. Her entire family was killed before her eyes that day and she was left alone in the boat out on the lake.

During the years following that traumatic event, she worked hard to put her life back together. Though she never had more children, she eventually married again. Her second husband, Wayne (not his real name), allegedly had a brief affair at one point in their marriage but they remained together. We met Betty and Wayne when we became the pastors of their home church.

By now, they were both in their 70's. She was a very sweet yet feisty little lady and Wayne was very kind and easygoing. About three years into our pastorate of this congregation, Betty was diagnosed with advanced, terminal cancer. She travelled all over the country to attend the healing services of televangelists. She was desperate to be healed. But no medical treatment or prayer helped and her cancer advanced to the point hospice was called in.

One day, while my husband was praying alone in the sanctuary at the church, the Lord spoke to him and told him that He would instantly heal this precious woman if she would surrender her anger and hurt to Him and choose to forgive herself (for her inability to rescue her family from the water) and God (for not sparing her of the tragedy). The Lord showed my husband that Betty not only had bitterness and unforgiveness toward herself and God for the death of her two little boys and their father, but was also harboring bitterness and unforgiveness toward Wayne for his alleged infidelity. After continuing to pray for her for a few days, my husband went to see her. At this point, hospice was with her and she was on her deathbed with her husband by her side. They were both happy to see their pastor walk through the door.

As he greeted them both, they were eager for him to pray for her. "Before we pray, I must tell you what the Lord spoke to me while I was praying for you these last few days," Pastor Jonathan began. "I believe the Lord said He will heal you if you will forgive. You must forgive yourself. You must forgive your first husband for not being able to save your boys that day. You must surrender the anger and bitterness you're holding against God Himself. And you must forgive Wayne. If you are willing to forgive, God will heal your heart and your body." "No," she retorted, "you don't understand. I cannot do that." At that point, my husband said she looked away and a darkness and hardness came over her face. Her mind was made up and she refused to budge. At that point, she began to writhe in pain and desperately and loudly gasp for air. Hospice was unable to bring relief. To the horror of everyone in the room, this went on for over an hour before she died. My husband said it was the most horrible death he's ever witnessed.

A short time after her death, her widowed husband had a garage sale. We stopped by to see if we could help in any way. We were surprised to see tables that were filled with brand new items; many still in the original boxes in which they were shipped. When Jonathan asked Wayne why he had so many brand new items for sale, Wayne explained that days before his wife's death, she callously confessed to him that, to get back at him for allegedly cheating on her (over 20 years earlier!), she had spent the last few months of her life ordering items from catalogs, infomercials, QVC, and other home shopping networks, in order to leave him in as much debt as she possibly could. She then hid the bills and merchandise from him. As physically ill as she was, she still managed to acquire over $20,000.00 of debt in his name! Wayne said, "Pastor, you were unaware of what she had been doing, but it made perfect sense to her and to me when you told her that she needed to forgive to receive healing."

## DO YOU SEE IT?!

Scripture is emphatic about the necessity of forgiving others. To be saved and to have intimate friendship with God, our Heavenly Father, forgiving others is not optional. When Jesus taught the disciples to pray, he made it unequivocally clear we must forgive to be forgiven:

*"After this manner therefore pray ye:*
*Our Father which art in heaven,*
*Hallowed be Thy name.*
*Thy kingdom come. Thy will be done*
*in earth, as it is in heaven.*
*Give us this day our daily bread.*
*And forgive us our debts,*
*as we forgive our debtors.*
*And lead us not into temptation,*
*but deliver us from evil:*

> *For Thine is the kingdom,*
> *and the power,*
> *and the glory,*
> *for ever. Amen."*
>
> Matthew 6:9–13 (KJV)

To reiterate the importance of forgiving others, Jesus elaborated in the verses that immediately ensued:

> *"For if ye forgive men their trespasses,*
> *your heavenly Father will also forgive you:*
> *But if ye forgive not men their trespasses,*
> *neither will your Father forgive your trespasses."*
>
> Matthew 6:14–15 (KJV)

Remember earlier when we expounded upon the unchanging, immovability of God? Isaiah 40:8 and 1 Peter 1:25 are references to the fact that God is immovable on this. Jesus, the pure and sinless Lamb of God, laid down His life to be sacrificed in able to offer us forgiveness for our sins. That cross was ours to bear. He selflessly took our place and forgave us while we were still sinners. How can we then selfishly refuse to forgive others when we ourselves are forgiven of so much?

We sinned against God and instead of holding it against us, He forgave us by sending His only, perfect son to pay the penalty for our offense against God. That penalty was death on a cross. He doesn't expect us to physically die on a cross for those who have sinned against us. But He does expect us to crucify our own bitterness, anger, and unforgiveness toward that person and forgive them. Forgiving others is not optional with God. We must walk in forgiveness to experience all that God has for us. Unforgiveness always blocks the power of God moving in our lives. Unforgiveness separates us from God and stops the flow of the divine supernatural in our lives. God said vengeance belongs to Him and that He alone can, and will, vindicate you. Unforgiveness is sin. God does not answer the prayers of Christians who abide in sin. (There's that word 'abide' again. I encourage you to go back to the definition and see how it relates to abiding *in sin* as well as *in Christ*.)

## BRING IT OUT OF THE DARK AND INTO THE LIGHT

There are several other sins, according to scripture, that will hinder our prayers. Psalm 66:17–18 sheds light on hidden sin:

> *"For I cried out to Him for help, praising Him as I spoke.*
> *If I had not confessed the sin in my heart,*
> *the Lord would not have listened.*
> *But God did listen! He paid attention to my prayer.*
> *Praise God, who did not ignore my prayer*
> *or withdraw His unfailing love from me."*

Confess and repent of the sin in your heart. If you don't know of any sin in your heart, ask God to search your heart and to show you of anything that is displeasing to Him. He knows what it is. And He desires to see you set free. He will shed light on the darkness in your heart, if you truly want Him to. Confess and repent (turn away from) whatever He shows you and He is faithful to forgive.

## LOVE KNOWLEDGE AND CHOOSE THE FEAR OF LORD

God will not answer the prayers of those who hate His knowledge and do not fear Him. Anyone, Christian included, who chooses to willfully abide in sin is clearly not choosing the fear of the Lord. Therefore, God will not listen to him and his prayers are hindered.

> *"When they cry for help, I will not answer.*
> *Though they anxiously search for Me,*
> *they will not find Me.*
> *For they hated knowledge*
> *and chose not to fear the Lord.*

*They rejected My advice and paid no attention*
*when I corrected them.*
*Therefore, they must eat the bitter fruit*
*of living their own way…"*
*Proverbs 1:28–31(NLT)*

*"If anyone turns a deaf ear to My instruction,*
*even their prayers are detestable to Me."*
*Proverbs 28:9*

*"Those who cling to worthless idols forfeit the grace that could be theirs."*
*Jonah 2:8(NIV)*

*"We know that God does not listen to sinners.*
*He listens to the godly person who does His will."*
*John 9:31*

*"The Lord is far from the wicked,*
*but He hears the prayer of the righteous."*
*Proverbs 15:29*

*"The eyes of the Lord watch over those who do right,*
*and His ears are open to their prayers.*
*But **the Lord turns His face against those who do evil**."*
*1 Peter 3:12*

*"But your iniquities have made a separation*
*between you and your God,*
*and your sins have hidden His face*
*from you so that He does not hear."*
*Isaiah 59:2*

I could write an entire book on this alone. This isn't a popular message in modern-american churches today. But it is truth. It is God's Word. And if we want to walk in freedom and in intimate friendship with God, we must take inventory of our attitude and choices and line them up with God's Word. Do you ignore wise instruction? For example, does your lifestyle consist of sexual immorality? Negative talk and gossip? A steady diet of junk? Too much stress and too little rest? Then you wonder why you're sick and God isn't healing you!

Are you actively reading/studying and obeying God's Word? Do you honestly desire to please Him in every area of your life? Do you have an attitude of thankfulness and gratitude? Do you avoid temptation for fear of displeasing Him? I'm not talking about doing everything perfectly in a legalistic manner, but rather having a heart that loves His Word and shudders at the thought of grieving God with a lifestyle that is contrary to His Word.

> *"Fear of the Lord is the foundation of true knowledge,*
> *but fools despise wisdom and discipline.*
>
> *Prov. 1:7*

## GOD WILL NEVER REJECT A BROKEN REPENTANT HEART

There is a big difference between flippantly disobeying God and genuinely struggling to break free from a sin that easily entangles you. That's the difference between those the Lord rejects and those He receives. God will never reject a broken and repentant heart (Psalm 51:17). No matter how many times you fall, a righteous man will run right back to the Father with a genuinely repentant heart (Proverbs 24:16). Those that love God will continue to pursue freedom from their sin by clinging to Christ and obeying His Word.

## DISHONORING YOUR SPOUSE HINDERS YOUR PRAYERS

According to scripture, how you treat your spouse can have a direct effect on whether or not God hears your prayers. 1 Peter 3:7

states clearly that if you are not treating your wife honorably God will not listen to your prayers. We must treat our husbands honorably with respect, just as the church, the body of Christ, respects Christ as the head.

> *"Husbands... be considerate as you live with your wives,*
> *and treat them with respect as the weaker partner*
> *and as heirs with you of the gracious gift of life,*
> *so that nothing will hinder your prayers."*
>
> *1 Peter 3:7 (NIV)*

If you're not sure how God expects husbands and wives to act toward one another, start with Ephesians 5:22–33 and 1 Peter 3. Real women serve, love and respect their husbands as the church loves Christ. Real men serve, love and respect their wives as Christ loves the church: tenderly and sacrificially.

## DISHONORING YOUR PARENTS OR NOT PROVIDING FOR YOUR CHILDREN

How we treat others matters greatly to God. Honoring and respecting God, and honoring and caring for others is the basis for the Ten Commandments.

> *"Honor your father and mother,*
> *so that you may live long in the land*
> *the LORD your God is giving you."*
>
> *Exodus 20:12*

This is the only one of the Ten Commandments' that comes with a promise: *a long life*. I'm not insinuating that all who have died young didn't honor their parents but it's certainly worth noting that God found honoring your parents important enough not only to command it, but promised to bless you in a special way for keeping that commandment. Honoring your parents does not mean being abused or controlled by an abusive, manipulative father or mother. And it does not mean obeying them at the expense of obeying God's commands. It simply means choosing to always be kind and respectful, not to bad-mouth them or purposefully neglect them when they are helpless and it's within your ability and power to help meet their genuine basic needs.

Furthermore, parents are charged by God to love, nurture, and discipline their children in the fear of the Lord. Children (like all of us) are a lot like bank accounts. In order to reap the blessing of a positive withdrawal of money, you must have first invested money into that bank account. Don't think you can demand obedience and respect from your children if you have not been investing your love, respect, time, affirmation, etc. into their hearts and lives.

*"...fathers, provoke not your children to wrath: but bring them up in the nurture and admonition of the Lord."*

*Ephesians 6:4*

*"Fathers, do not exasperate your children, so that they will not lose heart."*

*Colossians 3:21*

*"But if any provide not for his own, and especially for those of his own house, he hath denied the faith, and is worse than an infidel."*

*1 Timothy 5:8*

Do not think you can be a deadbeat dad or a deadbeat mom and expect to receive anything from the Lord.

## DOUBT AND DOUBLE-MINDEDNESS NULLIFY OUR PRAYERS

This is, in my personal observation, a major issue in the lives of 'believers'. We must take inventory of our belief system and get intellectually honest with ourselves about what we claim we believe and what we really believe. Without faith it is impossible to please God (Hebrews 11:6). Anyone who comes to Him in prayer, must believe wholeheartedly that God not only exists but that He rewards those that diligently seek Him. He tells us to stand firm in our faith, without wavering (Hebrews 10:23) because a double-minded person will be unstable in everything he does and will not receive anything from the Lord. Do you really believe or don't you? That question must be settled before you can move forward in faith to conquer the giants. We cannot afford to be full of faith one moment and trembling in unbelief the next. **That is why we must continually and consistently *abide* in His Word *and* in His presence**. Then, and only then, can we stand unwavering upon the truth of His Word, regardless of how we feel or how bad things get. We must not be moved by circumstances or the unreliability of our emotions. Our trust and faith is anchored in His promises found in His unfailing Word.

*"But he must must ask in faith without any doubting, for the one who doubts is like the surf of the sea, driven and tossed by the wind. For that man ought not to expect that he will receive anything from the Lord, being a double-minded man, unstable in all his ways."*

*James 1:6–7 (NASB)*

## HYPOCRITICAL PRAYERS WILL FALL FLAT

God isn't impressed with fancy, showy prayers prayed in public. What you are in private, when the preacher and the church folk aren't around, is who you really are. Putting on a big show of faith in church to impress people with how spiritual you are will never produce good fruit in your life. It's repulsive to God and trust me, it's repulsive to everyone around you. Pride, arrogance, and especially spiritual pride are like bad breath: everyone in the room knows you have it but you. Most Christians, if we're honest, have fallen prey to this pharisaical spirit on many occasions. You're not fooling anyone and you're certainly not fooling God. If you've fallen into this trap, confess it and repent of it. Humble yourself before God and man and He will honor you for it.

*"When you pray, don't be like the hypocrites*
*who love to pray publicly on street corners*
*and in the synagogues where everyone can see them.*
*I tell you the truth,*
*that is all the reward they will ever get."*

Matthew 6:5

## GOD HATES PRIDE AND RESISTS THE PROUD

You may be thinking this falls into the previous paragraph but pride applies to much more than just 'putting on a show in church'. Like I said before, oftentimes, pride is like bad breath, everyone in the room knows you have it but you. Ask God to reveal your pride to you. And if you dare to be teachable and can handle the truth, ask those that know you the most and aren't afraid to tell you the truth. Be willing to listen and not try to defend yourself. We all succumb to pride so don't take it too personally. However, just because everyone succumbs to it in one form or another, doesn't mean you can justify it.

Pride also raises its ugly head when we have embraced other sins. Instead of confessing our lifestyle as sin and repenting of it, we choose to wear it as a badge of honor. We brag about our sin in the locker room or march in the streets with banners. We drive the latest status symbol and make sure the designer label is on the outside of our shirt and purse so everyone knows how cool, powerful, or successful we are. We do our good works for all to see and make sure we get the credit when the credit is due to us. Some even take pride in being poor! Regardless of what our pride stems from, it not only displeases God, it angers Him.

Being humble doesn't mean we don't strive for excellence or that we can't enjoy nice things. Pride is *self* serving. Pride is a *"look at me"* attitude. Pride is being more focused on yourself than on God and others. Sometimes pride is thinly veiled fear or insecurity. And oftentimes, fear and insecurity are thinly veiled pride. Either way, they are displeasing to God. If you will humble yourself under God's mighty hand, He will lift you up in due time (James 4:10; 1 Peter 5:6). The world thinks pride goes hand-in-hand with power and freedom, but the truth is just the opposite. Humility is powerful and truly freeing!

*"One's pride will bring him low,*
*but he who is lowly in spirit will obtain honor."*
*Proverbs 29:23*

*"God opposes the proud, but gives grace to the humble."*
*James 4:6*

## FEAR: THE ANTITHESIS OF FAITH

One of Satan's most lethal weapons against us is the spirit of fear. This type of fear is not the healthy, God-given fear that says, *"don't touch that fire"* or *"don't step off the edge of a cliff"*. I'm talking about the demonic spirit of fear that disguises itself in many ways. Worry, fear and anxiety can overwhelm us with a dark shadow, controlling our every move and decision. There is always a plethora of reasons to be fearful. We fear wars, natural disasters, terrorism, riots and civil unrest, economic uncertainty, disease and death. We fear for our children's safety. We fear we won't have enough money. We fear being alone. We fear not being good enough, handsome enough, smart enough. The list is endless. Satan loves to paralyze us with this weapon called fear. And a powerful weapon it is. That is why knowing the truth of God's Word is so important. If we know the Truth, it will set us free from all fear. Fear is the antithesis of faith.

The words *"fear not"* appear 366 times throughout scripture. That's one for everyday of the year, including leap year! To the born-again believer, there is no fear in death. No fear in life. No fear of man. No fear of Satan. NO FEAR. No fear except the healthy, holy fear of grieving God, the Creator and Savior of our souls. An entire chapter could be devoted to this alone. If you are struggling with fear of any kind, I encourage you to confess it to someone whom you can trust to help you find freedom according to Scripture. Search out every Scripture concerning fear and every Scripture on who you are in Christ (google *"Scriptures on fear not"* and *"who I am in Christ"*). But for now, at least ponder the following truths from Scripture:

> *"So do not fear, for I am with you;*
> *do not be dismayed, for I am your God.*
> *I will strengthen you: yea, I will help thee: yea,*
> *I will uphold thee with the right hand of My righteousness.*
> *All who rage against you will surely be ashamed and disgraced;*
> *those who oppose you will be as nothing and perish...*
> *For I AM the LORD your God who takes hold of your right hand*
> *and says to you, Do not fear; I will help you...*
> *I Myself will help you."*
>
> *Isaiah 41:10–14*

> *"For God has not given us a spirit of fear and timidity,*
> *but of power, love, and self-discipline."*
>
> *2 Timothy 1:7*

> *"Behold, I give unto you authority to tread on serpents and scorpions, and*
> *over all the power of the enemy, and nothing will injure you."*
>
> *Luke 10:19*

## IGNORING THE NEEDY WILL HINDER YOUR PRAYERS

Proverbs 21:13 sums it up perfectly. Caring for those less fortunate must always be a part of our lifestyle. But Jesus, in Matthew 6, took it a step further than just being charitable. He said if we want to be blessed for our charitable acts, we must do it quietly, without a show.

> *"Whoever shuts their ears to the cry of the poor*
> *will also cry out and not be answered."*
>
> *Proverbs 21:13 (NIV)*

> *"But when you give to the needy,*
> *do not let your left hand know what your right hand is doing*
> *so that your giving may be in secret.*
> *Then your Father, who sees what is*
> *done in secret, will reward you."*
>
> *Matthew 6:3–4 (NIV)*

## WRONG MOTIVES AND UNGODLY PRAYERS

It's imperative we humbly examine our motives and our prayers to be sure they are not selfish but line up with the Word of God. We ultimately, as followers of Christ, must have this attitude of Christ in every situation, *"..not my will, but Thine be done.."* Everything we do in life should have the underlying goal of bringing honor, joy and glory to God.

> *"All a person's ways seem pure to them,*
> *but motives are weighed by the Lord."*
>
> *Proverbs 16:2 (NIV)*

> *"A person may think their own ways are right,*
> *but the LORD weighs the heart."*
>
> *Proverbs 21:2 (NIV)*

> *"When you ask, you do not receive,*
> *because you ask with wrong motives,*
> *that you may spend what you get on your pleasures."*
>
> *James 4:3 (NIV)*

## DIVINE MIRACLES SPAWN FROM DIVINE INTIMACY

This brings us back around to *abiding* in His presence. If we think we can pray for five or ten minutes a day and walk away a powerhouse for God, we will find out very quickly that is not the case. A nonexistent prayer life renders virtually nonexistent miracles. Certain divine miracles spawn from divine intimacy. When the disciples were perplexed as to why they could heal the sick but could not cast out a demon, Jesus told them, "..these come out only by prayer and fasting." The more we deny ourselves in order to abide in the presence of the Almighty God, the more His power will flow through us. That is a radical slap of reality in the face of today's watery, snowflake doctrine that is powered by the feelings and comforts of our minds and flesh. Many church leaders are preaching a false doctrine: that Christians can enjoy all the comforts of the flesh and the world while still serving Christ and walking in the power of His might. But there is absolutely nothing scriptural to that. It is not truth. It is a lie. Deception. Jesus was emphatically clear on this issue.

*"I am the vine, you are the branches;*
*he who **abides** in Me and I in him,*
*he bears much fruit,*
*for apart from Me you can do nothing."*
*John 15:5 (NKJV)*

*"If you **abide** in me and My Words **abide** in you,*
*ask whatever you wish, and it will be done for you."*
*John 15:7 (ESV)*

*"Trust in the Lord with **all** your heart*
*and lean not on your own understanding;*
*in **all** your ways **submit** to Him,*
*and He will make your paths straight."*
*Proverbs 3:5–6 (NIV)*

*"You desire but do not have, so you kill.*
*You covet but you cannot get what you want,*
*so you quarrel and fight.*
*You do not have because you do not ask God."*

*James 4:2 (NIV)*

We cannot *abide* in the culture of this world and *abide* in Christ (who is anti-culture; not of this world). The mindset of the world/culture is contrary to the mindset of Christ. And the mindset of Christ is contrary to the mindset of this world/culture that we live in. That's why scripture differentiates the two by explaining that while we live in this world we are not of this world (John 17:16). Pause for a minute and read Philippians 3. Remember, we are foreigners here. Our citizenship is in heaven (Philip.3:20), so come out from the world (2 Cor.6:17) and get into the presence of God. As you pray and study His Word, ask God to give you a heart that finds satisfaction in Him and not in the world. The payoff is eternally worth every effort. When we choose to participate in His suffering (by barring ourselves from sin and self, choosing instead to obey what He would ask of us), we are promised to share in His glory (resurrection power)! We are sons and daughters of God: joint-heirs with Christ. When we share in His suffering, we will share in the inheritance!

*"Though He (Christ) were a Son,*
*yet **learned He obedience by the things which He suffered**,*
*and being made perfect [complete],*
*He became the author of eternal salvation*
*unto all them that obey Him."*

*Hebrews 5:9 (AMP)*


## TAKING COMMUNION IN AN UNWORTHY MANNER

According to 1 Corinthians 11, *many* people in the church are weak, sick and spiritually asleep because they took communion in an unworthy manner and are guilty of sinning against the body and blood of the Lord.

> *"This is My body, which is for you; do this in remembrance of Me…*
> *This cup is the new covenant in My blood;*
> *do this, whenever you drink it, in remembrance of Me.*
> *For whenever you eat this bread and drink this cup,*
> *you proclaim the Lord's death until He comes.*
> *So then, whoever eats the bread or drinks the cup of the Lord*
> *in an unworthy manner will be guilty of sinning*
> *against the body and blood of the Lord.*
> *Everyone ought to examine themselves*
> *before they eat of the bread and drink from the cup.*
> *For those who eat and drink without discerning the body of Christ*
> *eat and drink judgment on themselves.*
> ***That is why many of you are weak and sick,***
> ***and a number of you have fallen asleep.***
> *But if we were more discerning with regard to ourselves,*
> *we would not come under such judgment."*
>
> *1 Corinthians 11:24–32 (NIV)*

Before you partake of communion, examine your life and scripture to be sure you take communion in a worthy manner. Here are 'unworthy' manners according to scripture (1 Corinthians 11):

- Taking communion without having surrendered your life to Christ's Lordship
- Partaking without complete, sacred respect and sober awareness that the elements (bread/wine) represent the sacrifice of Christ by which we are redeemed from sin
- Partaking while having an unresolved issue/offense with another believer (Mt.5:23)
- According to 1 Cor.11:21, some Corinthians were using the communion supper as an opportunity for self-indulgence, which is evidently how some got drunk

- Partaking of communion with willful, unconfessed sin
- Partaking of one of the elements and not both as Jesus modeled for the disciples

## HIS TIMING AND PLAN IS BETTER THAN YOURS

Rarely does God ever answer our prayers *when* we want and exactly *how* we want. Why is that? Because God sees everything from a different (right) perspective. He knows all—the past, present, and future, and is working all things for the good of those that love Him. Just because He doesn't answer right away, doesn't mean the answer isn't yes. It may be yes, but not right now. Trust that He is in control, He loves you, and He has something better for you than you have asked for. We are a lot like children looking at a parade through the knothole of a fence while God, our Father, is looking far above the fence seeing the entire parade from beginning to end. Like the child crying to the father, "Where are the clowns?! There are no clowns and I wanted to see clowns!!" The father encourages the child, "Be patient, the clowns are coming." Or perhaps the Father remains silent because he knows there is something coming that is even more exciting to the child than clowns could ever be. He knows the child is about to be wowed but the child, rather than waiting patiently, trusting that the father knows best, is full of anxiety and frustration because he can't see what he wants, when he wants.

> *"For My thoughts are not your thoughts,*
> *neither are your ways My ways,' declares the LORD.*
>
> *Isaiah 55:8 (ESV)*

> *"'For I know the plans I have for you', declares the Lord,*
> *'plans to prosper you and not to harm you;*
> *plans to give you hope and a future.'"*
>
> *Jeremiah 29:11 (NIV)*

*"Now to Him who is able to do exceedingly,*
*abundantly above all we could ask or think,*
*according to His power that is at work in us."*

*Ephesians 3:20 (NKJV)*

*"And we know that for those who love God,*
*all things work together for good,*
*for those who are called according to His purpose."*

*Romans 8:28 (ESV)*

## OPENING THE DOOR TO YOUR MIRACLE

As we have seen, there are several things that obstruct the flow of God's power in our lives to produce the miraculous:

- Rebellion against God
- Unforgiveness
- Prayerlessness/not abiding in Him
- Our own words/the declarations of our own lips
- Willful, hidden sin
- Dishonoring your spouse and/or parents
- Hypocrisy
- Pride
- Fear
- Lack of charity/making a show of our charity
- Wrong motives/ungodly prayers
- Taking communion in an unworthy manner
- His timing/His better plan

We must resist the temptation to over-complicate things. The Word of God is complex but not complicated. When we possess an attitude from the heart that genuinely wants God's will for our lives, He is faithful to guide us through to victory. No matter how incapable or weak you feel to overcome sin, that's when His strength will come to empower you to do the impossible. Here's the key: when we *daily* read His Word, *abide* humbly in His presence and pray *continually*, He will speak to us, guide us, empower us, and order our steps. He is for us and not against us when we live our lives to bring glory to Him (Romans 8:31). Don't let condemnation of your yesterdays ever keep you from all that God has for you today. *His steadfast love never changes, His compassions fail not and His mercies are new every morning* (Lamentations 3:22–23). When we confess and repent of our sins, the Bible says He is *Faithful and Just to forgive* us! He wants to bless you and to work His miraculous, beautiful plan in and through you. Grab ahold of His hand while you seek His face. He will lead you on the path of life and the journey will be exhilarating!

## PRAYER

"Heavenly Father, I truly desire to walk in spiritual freedom and in an intimate friendship with you. Oh LORD, my God, please search my heart and reveal any wicked way in me. [repent of each sin that the Holy Spirit brings to your mind]. Forgive me for not continually abiding in Your presence but rather walking in the desires of my own flesh and futile thinking. Create in me a clean heart and a right spirit that desires You more than gratifying my own flesh. Give me a deep love for Your Word; Your instruction, and Your presence in my daily life. Draw me into a life of abiding in You as I surrender my will, my time, my own knowledge, for the purity of Your Word and Your Holy Spirit working in me. Thank You that You reward those that diligently seek after You (Hebrews 11:6) and that my prayers are powerful and effective (James 5:16)!"

## FOR REFLECTION AND MEDITATION

### MEMORIZE John 8:31-32 (ESV):

*"If You abide in My Word, you are truly My disciples, and you will know the Truth, and the Truth will set you free."*

### MEDITATE

*Read and meditate on John 15: 1–2, 4–11.*

*Write down what the definition of abide is and let this verse sink deep into your soul. Post it where you can see it daily and begin putting it into practice.*

### MANDATE

*Read Matthew 6:9–13 & Mark 11:25–26. Forgive those that the Holy Spirit brings to your mind. Ask the Holy Spirit to set you free from the unforgiveness, hurt, and anger and to fill you with godly love for those who have hurt you or the people you love. Be sure to thank God for all He has forgiven you of.*

# Notes

*Chapter Five*

# CONQUERING CANCER [AND THE SPOILS OF WAR]

*"Now unto Him who is able to do exceedingly,*
*abundantly above all that we ask or think, according to*
*the power that worketh in us, unto Him be glory…"*

Ephesians 3:20 (NKJV)

*"…We are more than conquerors*
*through Him who loved us."*

Romans 8:37 (NKJV)

## WHAT ARE WE SO AFRAID OF?

IT WAS JANUARY of 2014 when I got the call from my friend, Linda (not her real name). With her voice breaking from crying, she could hardly speak. She had just left her doctor's office with the news that there was a lump on her breast and they needed to do a biopsy to determine whether it was cancer. She was terrified. Now Linda was a Christian and loved the Lord very much. I was quite perplexed at this dichotomy. On one hand, she was a strong follower of Christ who was quite knowledgeable in the Bible. On the other hand, she was absolutely consumed with fear. I thought about the fact that the Bible says, "God has not given us the spirit of fear" (2 Timothy 1:7), and yet so often, even as strong believers, we find ourselves securely bound within fear's paralyzing grip. For the next few weeks, I kept mulling this over in my heart, troubled by the obvious contradiction of thought. At the beginning of February (following my January conversations with Linda) I was speaking with a very close friend, Karen, who was talking about all the cancer in her family. Her father, mother, and many other close relatives had been diagnosed with cancer and many had died from it early in life. In the course of our conversation, she made the statement concerning her and her sisters, "I feel like we're just sitting ducks, waiting for our number to come up!" She's also a very strong Christian. Once again, I was troubled by the contradiction.

These phone calls really got me thinking about what the Bible has to say about these attitudes and what the ramifications are of such thought patterns. Once again, I was troubled by the contradiction. The Scriptures ran through my head, "We are more than conquerors in Christ Jesus" (Romans 8:37) and "As a man thinketh in his heart, so is he" (Proverbs 23:7). As Christians, we are not "sitting ducks" but as Paul puts it in 2 Corinthians, "Now thanks be to God, who always causes us to triumph in Christ...". I thought perhaps God wanted me to prepare a teaching on this subject to share with the group of ladies I meet with monthly for Bible study and to share when I speak at different events. I would encourage them with all the wonderful truths in God's Word that could alleviate their fears and infuse them with hope and power. But God had a totally different plan for these ladies...and for me!

## FROM RESEARCH TO REALITY

The following month, I decided to do some research on holistic approaches to some physical challenges I was experiencing. I figured I would also research what preventative measures could be taken to protect ourselves from this growing cancer epidemic. In the course of my research, I felt like God was telling me to do a 30-day juice fast. That did not sound the least bit desirable to me, so I decided to buy time by further researching. I researched juicing. I researched juicing machines. I researched juicing recipes. I researched until, I think, even Google was tired of it! Four months later, I finally took the plunge and bought the juicer. And in classic procrastination fashion, it sat on the kitchen floor, unopened, for weeks.

My husband finally decided to take this bull by the horns for me and one fateful Sunday morning, he made me a delicious glass of fresh carrot juice. I say delicious because it wasn't the absolutely disgusting flavor that I had anticipated! Of course, it was no choc-olate milkshake like I was secretly hoping, but it wasn't triggering my gag reflex, so I couldn't complain. I wasn't feeling well the night before and that morning. I was experiencing, abdominal pain and cramping. As the day progressed, the pain was steadily increasing. By early evening, I was in the worst pain of my life. Our family doctor came to the house to examine me. He said I needed to go to the emergency room but I kept thinking I could tough it out. I had heard of women who get cysts on their ovaries and they'll burst and bring relief. I had never had one, but thought maybe that was it. I have a very high tolerance for pain, so I thought I'd just endure until the relief came. It never came.

Even after our doctor had administered strong pain medication, the pain continued to escalate. I was literally writhing on the bed in pain. My precious little dog was on the bed beside me and would not leave my side. When I began writhing from the intensity, she started jumping off the bed, running out of the room and then running back in the room, jumping back on the bed and standing beside me. I was in so much pain I didn't really notice what she was doing until I felt something else next to me. When I looked to see what it was, I realized what she had been doing. She had brought all of her toys and laid them next to me in her eager attempt to console me.

Even in the midst of blinding pain, my heart was so touched at the tenderness and compassion of my furry little friend.

The pain quickly reached the point in which I felt as if it could possibly be life threatening, so I decided, in desperation, to go to the hospital. Needless to say, my doctor, husband and daughter were quite relieved I had finally surrendered my stubborn resistance to go. Off we headed to the Emergency Room.

After massive doses of their strongest painkiller, the pain was finally under control. Not gone, just under control. The source of the pain was determined: a large hematoma in the uterus. It would not have broken up or passed. Hence, the unbelievable and unrelenting pain. The head nurse in the ER, later told me, "I've been a nurse in this ER for over a decade and I've never seen anyone in as much pain as you were. The whole team of nurses were traumatized by it!" And this was the Woman's Hospital with pregnant women coming through daily with labor pains!

It sounds crazy (at least it did to me) but while I was in the middle of that intense pain, 1 Thessalonians 5:18 came to mind, "...in everything give thanks, for this is the will of God in Christ Jesus for you."

When you're experiencing pain this intense, all you can do is focus on being able to breathe. Your mind isn't wandering! It's laser focused. Only God could drop a Bible verse in your head at a moment like this. Especially one that says to give thanks! So, while breathing like a wounded animal, I began saying aloud, "Thank you, Lord. I give you praise. Thank you, Lord...!" I thought, *these people are going to think I've completely lost my mind!* But as I thanked Him, I felt supernatural strength from that moment on. Going from "God help me!" to "I thank you and praise you, Lord!" did something to me I can't explain. All I can say is, it was powerful and profound!

Once admitted, two different hospital staff doctors recommended I have a D&C. However, I didn't have a good feeling about it, so I told them I wanted to wait until my gynecologist arrived and

I could hear her assessment. Colossians 3:15 tells us "let the peace of Christ rule your hearts." I've learned over the years to listen and pay attention to what my "gut" tells me. Once again, it didn't fail me.

When my doctor arrived, she was quite relieved upon examining me to know I refused the D&C. She said it most likely would have punctured the uterus wall and caused severe complications. Thank God for the leading of His still, small voice! She told me I needed to schedule a complete hysterectomy immediately. Even though I had come to the hospital with the dogmatic attitude that I was not going to have a complete hysterectomy, I felt an undeniable, total peace about her recommendation. I agreed and surgery was scheduled for the following morning. Once again, it pays to listen to that peace, or lack thereof, that the Lord impresses in you.

## A WORD FROM GOD: LIVE IT OUT LOUD

When I had awakened from surgery the next day, the surgeon came in my room to give me the results. "Everything went great," he said, "The surgery was very successful, the abdomen is very clean now and all the tests came back negative." Then he continued, "However, while testing, the pathologist noticed a very small spot on the outside of each ovary that seemed a bit suspicious, so he's having them further tested to make sure it's nothing. We will have the results in a few days." I thanked the doctor and he was on his way.

Immediately, I felt the Holy Spirit speak to me and say, "The tests will come back positive but this is not unto death. And while this is about you, this is much bigger than you." I also felt Him say, "Live this out loud and I will be glorified through you". I felt challenged, but at peace. I knew God was on a mission and that I just needed to fully believe, trust, and obey. Had I insisted on only a partial hysterectomy (removing only the uterus) the cancer would not have been discovered.

When the Lord said to me, "…this is about you," I knew exactly what He was putting His finger on. My sugar addiction. I've been addicted to sugar since childhood. I've attempted many times through the years to break free from the grip of this intense addiction. I would cut out sugar, go on special diets, but could never succeed. Sugar addiction is ten times stronger than a heroin addiction.

A couple of days after being released from the hospital, I received the call from the doctor. My best friend, Debra, was visiting at the time the call came. With reluctance, he proceeded to tell me, "The tests came back positive for ovarian cancer." He continued to tell me about the gynecologic oncologist that he was attempting to connect me with. "He's the best and I'm making every effort to get you an appointment with him. He will know the best course of action for you." I smiled and thanked him for everything before hanging up. I think he must have thought I was in denial because I seemed so nonchalant about it. After all, ovarian cancer is no joke. My aunt, who had just retired from a career with the American Cancer Society, was very grieved to hear the report as she knew, unlike breast cancer and other cancers like it, ovarian cancer was "a whole 'nother level" of deadly.

I didn't feel anything but peace and confidence when he spoke the report of cancer to me. I knew my purpose on earth was not yet complete. When I hung up the phone, I told Debra the news. There were no tears and no fear; only peace and calm. I knew beyond a shadow of a doubt that God was in control and He had a purpose in this: to bring glory to His name.

After receiving the call, I knew that everyone was waiting to hear the report. I didn't want to tell my family. I didn't want them to be stressed or afraid. I also didn't want to tell friends and extended family because, honestly, I didn't want the attention nor drama that often ensues from such an awful report. But I knew, for God to get any glory, it had to be lived out loud. Growing up as a pastor's daughter of a large church, I learned, at a young age, to value any privacy and exclusivity I could get. Then, as an adult in pastoral ministry, you're used to the focus being on others' needs and I was good with that. 'Sheep' are always looking to the shepherd to be there for them in *their* time of need.

As much as I've been in the spotlight throughout my life (pastor's daughter, pastor's wife, pastor, public speaking, singing, television appearances, etc), I've never relished being in the public eye. I don't like the attention on me but rather my message. I know that sounds contradictory but let me attempt to explain. I've been singing solos in church since I was 5 years old. I loved singing all the time. It was a wonderfully fulfilling form of expressing and releasing the passion in my heart. I would even get in trouble in kindergarten and elementary school because I was always humming or singing to myself. It just bubbled up from within me. It had to come out. However, I always wished, when singing on stage, that I could hide behind a scrim to perform. I didn't want everyone looking at me. I just wanted to sing, to express the awesomeness of God for everyone to hear. When I was a young adult, this new way of singing in church was emerging. It was called "leading worship". Instead of just standing on stage performance style, "worship leaders" would lead the entire church into worshipping God through song. I loved it!

Finally, I could express my love and passion for God through singing, but the focus wasn't on me, it was on God as the entire congregation was focusing on Him, not me. I said all that to say, I greatly valued the support and prayers of friends and family, but was a little embarrassed at the attention brought on by this. It was very humbling for me to have such a private matter made so public.

While at home recuperating from surgery, Jonathan and I were praying about what the next step would be. I began feverishly researching ovarian cancer and its treatment protocols. Although the surgeon said the oncologist would most likely prescribe chemo-therapy, I didn't feel I was supposed to do it. The cancer was just beginning on the ovaries and they had removed it along with all my reproductive organs. I kept hearing in my mind, the words the surgeon had said after surgery, "We got everything and the abdominal cavity is very clean." Jonathan and I both felt that I wasn't supposed to do chemo but to do everything I could to heal holistically.

The day came for my initial consultation with the oncologist. His recommendation was 3 months/6 rounds of chemo to just make sure they got it all in surgery. Six rounds of chemo to make sure they got it all?! The doctor said that if I did nothing, I stood a 30% chance of recurrence and if it did recur, it would be incurable. Jonathan and I left the consultation very unsettled by his words. Even my best friend, Debra, who sat in the meeting with us, was disturbed by how the meeting went.

We took the next couple of weeks to think and to pray about it. Everyone had a strong opinion about what I should do. Most thought I should do the chemo. But Jonathan, Lexi, (our daughter) and I, all felt that I should forego the chemo for an holistic approach. The fact that Jonathan and Lexi felt as strongly as I did about doing no chemo held a lot of weight with me. Simple logic would deduce they ran the risk of losing their wife/mother if the cancer were to return.

Jonathan and I had been happily married 26 years at this point and have always shared an intensely deep love for one another. We weren't just husband and wife, but best friends. In more than one of our many discussions concerning whether to do chemo, he made the statement, "For you, 'to live is Christ, to die is gain.' That's a win-win for you. But if you die, I lose. I would be lost without you." (That's so sweet!) It was imperative to him that I live and yet he felt as strongly as I did that I should not do chemo. It's the whole "listen to that gut feeling" thing again. And so, after much prayer and discussion with family and friends, the only choice I felt peace about taking was the holistic route; then testing again in 6 months.

## RADICAL CHANGE

For the following six months, we radically changed my diet and lifestyle. We bought only organic food, installed water filters and air purifiers in our home, purged the house of all toxic household cleaners and toiletries. We quit using plastic containers of any kind and switched to glass and stainless steel. We disconnected the microwave and I turned my cell phone off at night and left it in another room. I drove into New Orleans as many days as I could to use the Photon Genius (a device that was said to help cure ovarian cancer). I cut sugar from my diet. I took supplements, consumed apricot seeds and did coffee enemas. I quit using candles, plug-ins, and air fresheners and started diffusing essential oils and applying them topically to my abdomen every day. Jonathan would juice 32 ounces of carrot/beet/spinach juice every morning before he left for work so I could drink it fresh each day. I consumed so much carrot juice, my skin literally turned orange! I searched out the scriptures on healing from the Word of God and prayed them over myself everyday. You name it, I did it. I was on a mission! After six months of this, it was time to test.

## TIME TO TEST

The first test I wanted to have done was a cutting edge test called the ONCOblot. With just a simple blood draw, it claims to detect, earlier than a scan, if there's cancer in the body and the point of origin. On the morning of my doctor's appointment to receive the ONCOblot test results, I was a mess on the inside. I'd had such peace through the previous six months. God had gone before me and led me with perfect peace. But fear had slithered its way in and I had no peace that morning, only a troubled spirit. I thought to myself, if the cancer is back, I would surely have missed God about doing chemotherapy.

I wasn't afraid of the cancer or even death, I was afraid I would have set up myself and my God to make us both look foolish; especially to unbelievers. I sat in my room pleading with God to help me feel His peace but nothing changed. Something in me just knew it wasn't going to be good and I needed His strength to handle it. Sure enough, the test was positive and the ovarian cancer was back. We immediately scheduled a scan.

I left the doctor's office feeling so defeated. I felt confused and embarrassed. God knew it would come back, so why, after so much prayer, didn't I feel any peace about doing chemo six months ago? And why did my family also feel so at peace about foregoing it? Could we all have been wrong? I felt ashamed and guilty. If I had just done what the doctor suggested, I wouldn't be putting my family through this now. And yet, I still felt so sure I had made the right choice. I was very conflicted and confused. When we step out in bold faith on something that we have no doubt God told us to do, it's inevitable we will have moments it appears we were dead wrong. There are so many examples of this in scripture. Take Moses and the Israelites for example. After exiting Egypt to "freedom", they instead found themselves in a death trap. With the most powerful army in the world in hot pursuit behind them and the uncrossable Red Sea before them, they knew (in the natural) they were toast. But God knew the end from the beginning and it was the exact set-up He had orchestrated to demonstrate His power to deliver His help-less sheep and destroy the biggest power on earth! Several times in scripture, the Lord commands us to "*stand firm*" and trust Him; to "*be still and know*" He is bigger than the crazy moment you find your-self in. This was one of those moments for me. Although I thought I had escaped its grip on me, this powerful and extremely aggressive cancer was back; attempting to seize and kill me even though God had given me very specific instructions (that I had followed to the best of my ability). But now, it appeared I had completely failed. Remember, the oncologist had told me that if the cancer returned, it would most likely be incurable.

The following day, I sat in the radiology department, waiting for the radioactive sugar to pump through my body for the awaited scan. While sitting there in that isolated room, I read the scripture my dear friend, Shelli, had texted me early that morning (she per-sonalized it just for me):

*'Because Salli holds fast to Me in love, I will deliver her; I will protect her, because she knows My name. When she calls to Me, I will answer her; I will be with her in trouble; I will rescue her and honor her.'*

*Psalm 91:14–15 (ESV) (Paraphrased)*

At that moment, as I read that scripture over and over, I felt my mind and spirit transforming. In place of the confusion, shame, guilt, and fear, I felt the resulted fog clear, His truth shine through and the warmth of His peace radiating within me once again. I didn't have an explanation for anything but I had a peace that He was in control of it all. My joy returned as I felt a tenacious resolve rise up within me to not waiver in what I knew God had told me. Consequently, I sailed through the scan and the wait for the results.

Even though it didn't make any sense, I still felt I had made the right choices and they were all working together as a set up for God to be glorified. Having exhausted my holistic options at this point, it was going to be divine intervention or a tragedy. My joy returned. I sailed through the test *and* the wait for the results.

A few days later, I was returning home from a ladies' bible study. It had been a glorious evening with my precious sisters-in-the-Lord. We had a wonderful evening of fellowship, study of the Word, and prayer. I always leave so full in my spirit after our times together. It was about 10:00 p.m. when I arrived home. I walked through the door to find my husband and my doctor sitting in the living room with a piece of paper lying in front of them on the coffee table. I knew instantly it was the scan results on the table and based upon their expressions and the fact the doctor was at my home at 10 o'clock at night, it wasn't good. However, I was unphased. I *knew* God was in control and we were on a mission. Whatever He had planned, His grace was sufficient. Sure enough, the cancer was definitely back. The scan showed two large masses in my abdomen and I would need to have surgery right away.

## CAROLING OUTSIDE HEAVEN'S GATE

The night before my surgery, we went to our dear friends' house for a party. At one point in the evening, we gathered around their beautiful grand piano to sing and worship God before they prayed for me. Like I've said, I don't like drawing attention to myself, and especially in small settings like this, I always felt quite self-conscious singing in front of people. But tonight was different. Heaven seemed closer to me than ever before. I could feel God's presence so strongly.

We knew the cancer was back with a vengeance. Who knew what all was in store. Either they would find me too advanced to even attempt to surgically remove it or they would remove it and I would have to do extreme rounds of chemo. For that matter, if I was wrong about it not being unto death, I could even die on that operating table the next day. Whatever tomorrow held, I had tonight. If it was my last night on earth, I was going to make it a symphony of worship and praise to my God. He had been my best friend for 48 years and I couldn't think of anything better than to sing about His love for me and my love for Him, with every ounce of strength I had.

For the first time in my life, I didn't care who was looking or what they thought. One of the most beautiful offerings we can give to God this side of heaven is to worship Him with all our hearts. When we get to heaven and behold Him in all His glory, we won't be able to help but worship Him. His awesome Glory will provoke it. This life is our only chance throughout all of eternity, to worship Him by faith. What must that do to the heart of God to see and hear us worshipping the God we have never seen with our eyes but only felt in our hearts. It is the beautiful, tangible substance of our faith being made evident. A faith that, according to Hebrews 11, is counted to us as righteousness.

While singing that evening, it was like caroling outside of heaven's gate. What a glorious experience! With my arms in the air and my face toward heaven, I was so caught up, I didn't even think about who might be looking. The Holy Spirit was all over me and my heart was bursting with love and gratitude for my Savior, Friend and King.

After our time of worship, my friends and family gathered around me to pray. A wonderful Christian man, who is also a medical doctor, led the prayer. I knew he was praying for me but I don't remember anything he said. Through the whole prayer, all I could whisper is "Lord, give me souls. Give me souls for this trial. Don't let this trial be wasted. Please, give me souls." Psalm 2:8 says, "Ask of me, and I shall give thee the heathen for thine inheritance…" The only thing we can take to heaven is people. It was burning within me for God to somehow use this fiery trial in my life to draw others to salvation in Christ; that they may know the joy of friendship with God like I had known since I was just a child.

## WORSE THAN THEY ANTICIPATED

The surgery lasted hours longer than originally approximated. The cancer had come back with a vengeance. Not only were there two large masses, it was in the appendix and all throughout the omentum wall (where the lymph nodes are). Furthermore, it was also what they called a *"seeding of the abdomen"* or as the oncology surgeon explained it in lay-terms: it was "smattered, like granulated sugar dropped on a hard floor, throughout the entire abdominal cavity". They got as much as they could, but the doctor said they could not get it all. A couple of the doctors expressed their shock at how the cancer had spread at such an unusually aggressive rate.

When my father-in-law (a retired physician) heard the report, he knew what it meant. Though he said nothing at that time, he later told us, "I've got to be honest with you, when I heard and saw the report, I knew it was your death sentence. I didn't see any way, medically, you could survive this. I wanted to tell Jonathan and your kids they needed to prepare themselves for the worst, but couldn't bring myself to say it."

## PEACE THAT PASSES UNDERSTANDING

However, even upon waking, and hearing the surgeon's report, I was at peace. The one thing I never doubted was that God had said it was not unto death. Though I thought I had missed God about not needing to do chemo, I knew with unshakable doubt that the Lord said I was not to die from this. I knew that wasn't just wishful thinking because I wasn't afraid to die but rather to the contrary; I was gladly ready to accept my promotion from this life to heavenly realms, even excited at the prospect! But I *knew* God was up to something. He had a divine purpose for this diagnosis and death was no part of it. He had handed me a mission, should I choose to accept it and allow Him to be glorified through it.

However, I also knew how I handled the whole situation would play a huge role in whether or not I would survive. Just because God had spoken to my heart that it was not unto death didn't mean He wasn't requiring anything on my part to see this promise come to fruition. I knew He was expecting me to fight in faith for it. As I pondered my healing as a child, I knew God was able to do the impossible. But I did nothing as a baby to see that come about; my parents did the work. They were the ones who sought out medical wisdom, prayed, fasted, held fast to the promises in God's Word, obeyed His every command. I was just the recipient. But this time, *I* was the adult. The baton was passed to me. And this time, I was the one who had to "fight the good fight of faith" to see the promise come to be.

*'Did I really have the faith to do this?'*, I thought. Because, ultimately, when you're in a fiery trial like this, no matter how many friends and loved ones you have supporting you, it still comes down to *your* choices in the matter. To settle this question, I had to search my heart and my belief system. These were some of my thoughts on the path of deductive reasoning as to whether I could do this:

- I obviously have seen supernatural miracles take place in others as well as myself. God's Word says He's no respecter of persons; what He's done for one, He'll do for others.

- I do believe in God.
- I believe the Bible is the inspired Word of God. That Word says, "...by His stripes, I am healed; He sent His Word and healed them; all things are possible to those that believe; He is an ever-present help in our time of need...The gospels said Jesus healed everyone He came in contact with so it seems pretty obvious between His Word and His actions, it's His desire all be healed." So, I concluded in thought,
- *'What do I have to lose by taking Him at His Word and stepping out in faith and believing it? Perhaps I will witness God and His power at work in me like never before!'*

The more I meditated on His Word and the past miracles I had witnessed and experienced, a fiery tenacity began rising up within me with powerful force. I knew in that moment, I was going to fight the fight of faith with all my heart, all my mind, and all my strength and to believe God to be all that He says He is and to do all His Word says He can do. At that point, I no longer cared what anyone else thought. This was between me and my God. And I was determined not only to hold His feet to the fire by reminding Him of His covenant promises to me, but hold my own feet to the fire of testing my own willingness to believe unwaveringly in the face of the impossible and moments of weakness. I also knew it was imperative that, no matter what happens, like David, I must keep my focus on the size of my God, not on the size of my giant enemy. The following verse was a major player in my fight:

*"My son (daughter),* **give attention *to My Words,* incline your ear** *to My sayings.* **Do not let them depart** *from your eyes;* **keep them** *in the midst of your heart;* **for they are life to those who find them and health to all their flesh."**

*Proverbs 4:20–22 (NASB) ('daughter' added)*

So I kept the Word of God within arm's reach at every moment through this trial. I had handwritten notes taped everywhere with healing Scriptures. I played Christian music continually. I had a little book containing the promises of God that I carried with me everywhere I went. I read (more than once!) Dodie Osteen's little booklet on her testimony of divine healing. I had the Bible app and Scripture lists on my phone so I would have quick access no matter where I was. Often, I would turn on the audio from the Bible app while lying in bed sick (day and night) and just listen to the Word of God for hours on end. I found the most comfort listening to the Gospels of Christ (Matthew, Mark, Luke, and John) and the Epistles of Paul (13 books in the Old Testament written by the Apostle Paul). The only thing I watched on television throughout the six month trial was the Andy Griffith Show because it was funny and wholesome; and laughter is good medicine.

## DRINKING DEADLY POISON

Two weeks after surgery, I began chemotherapy. After six months of living such a clean, non-toxic lifestyle, I cringed at the thought of pumping something so toxic into my body. But I knew it had to be done. I hadn't told anyone but I was a little scared and concerned about the chemo "burning" me internally; especially all the internal places still not healed from surgery. The night before my first chemotherapy treatment, my sister, Terri, called me. She told me that she was leaving church and a woman from their congregation hurried over to her to tell her something. The woman said, "Terri, God woke me up in the night to pray for your sister, Salli. The Lord gave me this Scripture to give her. Will you please give this to Salli?" I was blown away when Terri quoted the Scripture to me: *"When you walk through the fire, you will not be scorched, nor will the flame burn you."* (Isaiah 43:2b). Wow! God knew the fear that I had shared with no one. Immediately, the fear left.

I also grabbed ahold of Mark 16:18 that says, *"...and if they drink any deadly poison, it shall not harm them.."* I would take communion before each chemo session and would plead the blood of Jesus to cover and protect my body. I would also pray over the I.V. bags containing the chemotherapy drugs, that the drugs would only kill the cancer and not harm my body in any way. I continued to stand firm, quoting and believing the promises of God, that:

*"I shall not die, but live and declare the works of the Lord."*
*Psalm 118:17 (KJV)*

*"He sent His Word and healed me and delivered me from all my destruction."*
*Psalm 107:20 (paraphrased)*

*"O Lord, my strength, and my stronghold; and my refuge*
*in the day of affliction."*
*Jeremiah 16:19 (Amp)*

*"You are my hiding place and my shield;*
*I hope in Your Word."*
*Psalm 119:114 (ESV)*

*"For I will restore life to you and heal you of your wounds..."*
*Jeremiah 30:17(NKJV)*

*"In the beginning was the Word, and the Word was with God and the Word was God (John 1:1) and the Word became flesh and dwelt among us (v14) [and that flesh] was wounded for our transgressions, He was bruised for our iniquities; the chastisement for our peace was upon Him, AND BY HIS STRIPES WE ARE HEALED."*
*Isaiah 53:5(KJV)*

(These are just a sampling of the scripture verses I continually stood firm upon. I have them all listed for you in a quick reference section at the back of this book.)

If you have never read the Bible, much less, memorized passages from it, I can't urge you enough to do so. It's not just a historical book. It's *"alive and active."* It's the very words of God to all mankind.

> *"For the word of God is living and active, sharper than any two-edged sword, piercing to the division of soul and of spirit, of joints and of marrow, and discerning the thoughts and intentions of the heart... Since then we have a great High Priest who has passed through the heavens, Jesus, the Son of God, let us hold fast our confession. For we do not have a high priest who is unable to sympathize with our weaknesses, but One who in every respect has been tempted as we are, yet without sin. Let us then with confidence draw near to the throne of grace, that we may receive mercy and find grace to help in time of need."*
>
> *Hebrews 4:12, 14–16 (ESV)*

## THE TRUE SOURCE OF UNSHAKABLE PEACE AND STRENGTH

This passage in Hebrews sums up the secret to my strength, confidence, joy, and peace throughout this trial. **Jesus is the Word of God** made manifest in the flesh (John 1:1) and though He died on a cross as a sacrifice for our sins (2 Corinthians 5:21) , He was resurrected on the third day thereby conquering death, hell, and the grave for us. **He is alive** (1 Corinthians 3 & Revelation 1:8) and is *"...our Refuge and Strength; an Ever-present help in our time of need." (Psalm 46:1).* Because I have surrendered my heart and life to Him, His Spirit is now living in me (Revelation 3:20), which empowers me *not to worry about anything; instead, to pray about everything.* I tell God what I need, and thank him for all he has done. I experience God's peace, which exceeds anything we can understand. His peace then, *guards my heart and mind as I **live** in Christ Jesus'. (Philippians 4:6–7)*

## GOING FOR THE SPOILS OF WAR

As previously mentioned, when I was first diagnosed, after the hysterectomy, I felt God had spoken to my heart and told me this diagnosis of cancer was not unto death. As I pondered this promise in my heart, I thought about the passage of Scripture in Romans 8:37 that says, *"...now in all these things, we are **more** than conquerors through Christ Jesus..."* I thought about the health challenges I had been living with the last two decades: adrenal fatigue and hypothyroidism, a MTHFR gene mutation along with several herniated discs in my back and neck. I thought to myself, "Okay, the Lord told me I won't die from this cancer so, through Christ, I'm *going* to conquer it. But the Bible says I'm *more* than a conqueror. Even in the Old Testament, when God conquered and gave them victory over their enemies, they also 'took the spoils of war'." (Read 2 Chronicles on this epic battle!) So I thought, "If I'm *more* than a conqueror in Christ, than I'm asking Him for the *'spoils of war'.* I don't just want healing from cancer, I want total healing. No more adrenal fatigue, no more hypothyroidism, no more back/neck injury and I want a new kidney (again)!" (The pet scan had revealed one of my kidneys had atrophied. They believe this was a result of the blunt force trauma from the same car accident that injured my neck and back.)

John 16:24 says to ask that your joy may be full! Now God will choose, according to my greater good, what to do with those requests. He can heal it all or heal none of it. Either way, I know He's working it all for the best in my life and for others. Sometimes, God leaves something in our lives that we pray for him to remove. But in His Sovereignty, *He* knows what's best, not us. The Apostle Paul prayed three times for God to remove the 'thorn in his flesh' but God would not. This is a very telling passage:

> *"If I wanted to boast, I would be no fool in doing so, because I would be telling the truth. But I won't do it, because I don't want anyone to give me credit beyond what they can see in my life or hear in my message, even though I have received such wonderful revelations from God. **So to keep me from becoming proud, I was given a thorn in my flesh**, a messenger from Satan to torment me and keep me*

*from becoming proud. Three different times I begged the Lord to take it
away. Each time he said, 'My grace is all you need. My power works
best in weakness.' So now I am glad to boast about my weaknesses, so
that the power of Christ can work through me. That's why I take pleasure in my weaknesses, and in the insults, hardships, persecutions, and
troubles that I suffer for Christ. For when I am weak, then I am strong."*
*2 Corinthians 12:6–10 (NLT )*

When I came home from the hospital, following the hysterectomy,
I began praying healing Scriptures over my body; the abdomen where
the cancer was, my thyroid, my kidneys and adrenals, my back and
neck, everything! I would lay my hand on each spot and command it
to line up with God's Word, quoting the healing Scripture promises.
I remembered that God had spoken to me around Thanksgiving of
the previous year, that this would be an Ephesians 3:20 year for me.

*'Our God is able to do exceedingly abundantly more than I could
ask or think according to His power at work in us.'*
*Eph.3:20 (paraphrased)*

So, with faith and enthusiasm, I prayed and believed for complete healing. The natural reality, however did not immediately manifest this spiritual reality. I was sick as a dog from the chemo. The
chemo was not only administered intravenously but also through
an intraperitoneal 'port' device in my abdomen that would pump
the chemo directly into the entire abdominal cavity. The pain was
so intense in the abdominal cavity, the few days following chemo, I
could barely walk; when I did, I was bent over and could only slide
my feet as gently as possible. But I continued to stand firm in faith
and "...*call those things that are not as though they were...*" (Romans 4:17).

## AN UNEXPECTED HEALING: THE BODY OF CHRIST

Meanwhile, God was giving my family another healing. Over
the previous 10 years or so, my family had experienced tremendous

hurt and devastation at the hands of Christians and the church. We lost almost everything because of it—our home, car, retirement, friends, and reputation. The wounds inflicted through the rejection, betrayal, and lies spoken of us went deep into the core of all four of us. We understood, first hand, the pain that Joseph experienced at the hands of his brothers, when they rejected him and threw him away because of their hateful jealousy of the father's favor upon their brother (Genesis 37). Even though we continued to go to church (Hebrews 10:25) and persevere through it, there was still much need for healing. But God watched it all from His throne. He saw that, in spite of it all, we desperately fought everyday to keep our hearts free of bitterness and unforgiveness. And He is a rewarder of those that truly seek to love their persecutors from a pure heart. What seemed like the nail in our coffin, God was instead going to use this cancer trial to bring more than just miraculous healing in my body. He was about to show my little family what Christ's love, being made manifest through His church, truly looked like.

From day one of this cancer trial, God began showing us the love of the true church. They were at the hospital for my surgeries and every emergency room visit. They sent prayers and encouraging words of love through texts, Facebook, cards, phone calls, and flowers. They sat with me through chemo sessions and took me to doctor appointments. They held fundraisers and sent money. They cleaned our house. They brought meals and meals and *more* meals! It averaged out to a meal every other day for six months! My mother, who had been a pastor's wife for forty years kept saying to me, "This is unreal! I've never seen anything like this! I wouldn't believe it if I wasn't seeing it for myself! This just blows me away!" The love of God, being made manifest through the body of Christ (aka; *the* church) showed up and showed off! And it wasn't coming from one 'church', but from Christians everywhere.

People were coming out of the woodwork to love and support us. Some we had never even met. Friends I hadn't seen or talked to for over 30 years were fasting and praying for me and sending money and encouraging notes. Christians from every corner of the country and beyond rose to the occasion. They lavished my family with an overwhelming outpouring of the most sincere, tender and compassionate love of Christ. Our hearts melted and the wounds, deep below the surface, were being nursed and healed with every act of loving concern and generosity. It truly was the beginning of God blessing my little family *"exceedingly abundantly more than we could ask or think"*!

## THE MESSAGE WITHOUT WORDS

Not only were they a huge blessing to us, but I realized God was using me to show women everywhere what it looks like to walk above the fear and in the perfect peace that only the knowledge of God's truths and intimacy with Christ can bring.

It wasn't a sermon He wanted me to preach with my mouth but with my life through this trial. Cancer is one of people's biggest fears but there is no fear in Christ Jesus. No matter how hopeless or terrifying our circumstance may appear to be, God is bigger than it all.

When we really grasp that spiritual reality, and the solid understanding of who God is and who we are *in* Christ, we can walk in the same confidence David had when he went up against Goliath (1 Samuel 17) and the same courage and boldness the New Testament believers had when facing beatings, imprisonment, and martyrs' deaths.

Our lives are not our own when we accept Christ as our Lord and Savior. We belong to Him, not to ourselves. His desire is to draw others to Himself through us. When we make Him the most important part of our daily lives, obeying His leading at every turn, there's no limit to what He can do in us and through us. It doesn't mean we won't experience really tough trials. Psalm 34:19 says, *"Many are the afflictions of the righteous, but the LORD delivereth him out of them all."* God doesn't give us an easy life, He gives us a life filled with impossibilities so that we will allow His supernatural power to be made manifest through us for the world to see! He's given us every tool and truth we need to live that kind of life. He assured us of this over and over throughout Scripture:

> *"With men this is impossible, but with God,*
> ***all*** *things are possible."*
> *Matthew 19:26 (KJV)*

> *"Listen carefully:* ***I have given you authority*** *[that you now possess] to tread on serpents and scorpions, and [the ability to exercise] authority* ***over all the power of the enemy*** *(Satan); and nothing will [in any way] harm you."*
> *Luke 10:19 (AMP)*

> ***Confess your sins*** *to each other and* ***pray for each other*** *so that* ***you may be healed****. The* ***earnest prayer of a righteous person has great power*** *and produces wonderful results".*
> *James 5:16 (NLT)*

> *And I, if I be lifted up from the earth,*
> *will draw all men unto Me."*
> *John 12:32 (KJV)*

These are just a taste of the feast of Scriptures reiterating the power we are given to overcome *all* things and glorify God in the process. I could list fifty Scriptures here! See the Scripture reference guide at the end of this book. I strongly urge you to dive into Scripture to find every verse you can about who you are in Christ. It will have the potential to radically change your life. Meanwhile, back to the journey at hand...

## THE DARKEST HOUR IS RIGHT BEFORE THE VICTORY

It was six long months of bittersweet: the sweetness of Christ and His body (the Church) mixed with the nightmare of intense chemo and my *very* sick body.

During the fifth and sixth months of my treatments the enemy came in like a flood. I believe he was so angry at all that God was doing through this trial. Satan comes like a thief to steal, kill, and destroy (John 10:10) but instead, God was being glorified through this fiery trial in so many ways. So, the devil decided to step up his attack, hoping to abort all that God was giving birth to in all of our lives. Revelation 12:10 tells us that one of Satan's names is *"accuser of the brethren"* and that's exactly who showed up.

For weeks all I could hear was this demonic voice in my head sneering, *"God hates you! God HATES you!"* It was especially strong deep in the night hours. It was as if I could see, in my mind's eye, Satan, lining up on a mantle, these jar-like vessels that contained all the terrible trials we had been through. He was pointing at them and sneering, *"Look! Just LOOK at all that's happened these last ten years and tell me that God doesn't hate you. He hates you!"* The accusations were so strong it put me in a fetal position. I couldn't get away from it. All I could do is say over and over, *"Jesus! Jesus! Jesus, help me!"* In order to get any relief, I would put my headset on and either play worship music or an audio Bible all night. Even in the daytime, there was no relief.

Between being so weak and sick, the chemo messing with my brain at the same time every month (inducing nightmares), not being able to sleep, and being bombarded with this, I was desperate for relief. In my desperation, I cried out to God to show me how to break free from this. Because I couldn't get away from it, I began searching my own heart. Sometimes we can give Satan a crack in the door to come in because of sin in our lives. Genesis 4:7 tells us that if we do not do what we know is the right thing to do, *"sin is crouching at the door, eager to control you. But you must rule over it"*.

Sure enough, I knew what it was. A couple years earlier, in an important conversation, I told a lie. It was "just an insignificant" lie that hadn't made any difference to the situation; or so I had convinced myself of that. When asked if I had done something I was supposed to do, I told them yes when the truth was no. But that was beside the point. The point is, it was a lie. It was one of those sins that my conscious and the Holy Spirit would bring to my mind at random times but I would quickly justify not obeying the conviction of the Holy Spirit by convincing myself I would make the call…later. I wanted to call to tell them the truth but was embarrassed and afraid to.

Satan can really debilitate and entangle us with fear and that's just what he had done. "It's not a big deal. No one will ever even know the truth. And it doesn't affect anyone anyway. If you go back and tell them you lied, it will just hurt your reputation with them. How can that be a good thing?" Satan chimed in my ear, "And it's not like it even changes anything!" He concluded. When I told the lie, I was terribly convicted about it. But I put it out of my mind as much as I could and kept telling myself it really wasn't a big deal anyway and I would deal with it later. Though over a year had passed, I still hadn't set the record straight. I knew that little lie had given the enemy an open door into my life and I knew to be free from his torment, I would need to confess my sin to the right person and repent to God, no matter the cost. But I was so weak and sick and knew I didn't have the strength to rectify the situation immediately. So, I made a vow to God that as soon as I had the strength, I would do it. This time I meant it. I asked forgiveness and the tormenting spirit left.

As believers, there is no place for deliberate sin in our lives, no matter how small, or even when it's a knee-jerk reaction that we can justify. Sin is sin. We cannot justify it away and think God will do the same. His Word is clear. *"The **pure** in heart will see God." (Matthew 5:8). "Confess your sins to each other and pray for each other so that you may be healed." (James 5:16)* and *Revelation 21:8* clearly tells us liars will go to hell. He is longsuffering and merciful and will give us many opportunities to come clean but He still demands holiness and at some point we tie His hands from moving in our lives until we obey.

As soon as I had my strength, I made that phone call and confessed my sin. What a wonderfully freeing feeling that ensued. I don't know why I waited so long to do the right thing but I was thrilled it was done. If we want all that God has for us, we must keep our hearts clean. Don't get me wrong, God knows you will fail. It's not about perfection, it's about obedience and repentance when we do sin. Psalm 51:7 assures us that God will not reject a broken and repentant heart. And Proverbs 1 makes it clear that God will bless the person who walks in the fear of the Lord. His Spirit empowers us to walk holy *and* to confess and to repent when we don't. Not every attack like this one is a result of sin, but in this case, my sin had left me vulnerable to attack. First Peter 5:8 tells us to *"be sober, be vigilant; because your adversary the devil, as a roaring lion, walketh about, seeking whom he may devour"*. Life isn't a game, it's a battle; a battle for your soul. If we don't *"fight the good fight of faith"* (1 Timothy 6:12), we will get waylaid by our enemy. We fight with obedience to God through the power of the Holy Spirit in us. God then defeats our enemies and gives us *"... life and life more abundantly."* (John 10:10).

It was six long months of bittersweet; the sweetness of Christ from His body mixed with the nightmare of chemo and my very sick body.

The sixth month and last two sessions of chemo had arrived. I was so sick, they had to give me a blood transfusion and postpone both sessions by several days because my white and red cell counts were so low. But we finally finished with the last chemo session on November 9, 2015, followed by the usual 2 weeks of ill effects from the drugs. When I asked the oncologist what was next, after completing chemo, he said that I would need to do six more months of *weekly* (I.V.) lower-dose chemo. I was so disheartened at just the thought of that. My particular chemo was such an aggressive beast and I wouldn't wish it on my worst enemy.

Thanksgiving was just three days away as we loaded the car and headed to M.D. Anderson Cancer Center in Houston for testing. In my heart, I was still waiting to see Ephesians 3:20 fully manifested. It was a year since God had put that in my heart. The outpouring of love through the past year was amazing and I was so very grateful! But with three surgeries, six months of intense treatment, tens of thousands of dollars of medical bills piled high and my body ravaged by this beastly ordeal, I knew there had to be more blessing in store. And there was. *Much* more!

## NO EVIDENCE OF DISEASE

Praise God, the tests at MDA showed I was cancer free. And, the oncologist there said I didn't need any maintenance follow up treatments. I was so relieved but was very curious to see what my oncologist back home would say as he was confident I would need the six months of maintenance chemo.

The following week, I went to see my oncologist to share my results with him. I said nothing of what the doctor at MDA told me. He looked over the test results and was quite pleased. He told me I am, what they refer to as, N.E.D.—"No Evidence of Disease". I asked, "So, I assume that means I'm considered in remission?" He replied, "No! Remission means it's still there, lying dormant. You have *No Evidence* of Disease." Praise God! I asked him about doing the six months of maintenance and he said I didn't need it; I could go, enjoy my life. Just come back for a check up in 3 months. (Insert major happy dance here!!)

## THE SPOILS OF WAR

That would be a great ending in itself, but that's not the end of this story. The following day, I made an appointment with our family doctor to have bloodwork done to check everything (my vitamin/nutrient levels, red and white cell counts, thyroid, kidney, bone marrow count, liver function, etc). A good friend had gone through much less chemo more than a year prior to me and her white and red blood cell counts were still low over a year later; and she was still struggling with fatigue. I needed to know one of two things: was my body damaged from all it had endured or did God heal me completely like I'd been praying for. It was only 26 days after my twelfth round of chemotherapy when I had this blood profile drawn. In spite of having been so sick just two weeks earlier when my red and white cell counts were in the tank (and *very* anemic), I was now feeling amazing. I thought maybe it was just some kind of post-chemo high.

It was December 23rd, the day before Christmas Eve when I went back in for the results, accompanied by my son, Jay. Dr. May began by tenderly asking how I was feeling, assuming I was still feeling the detrimental effects. "I actually feel amazing!" I said energetically, "In fact, I literally feel better than I've felt in decades!" His face gave way to surprise and disbelief as he said, "Well, you certainly look and sound great. Let's look at your bloodwork."

He had not read the lab results prior to this. "Let's just start at the top," he said, as he began to read aloud while pointing out each line with his fingers. "Your red cell count is perfect. Your white cell count is perfect. There's no anemia…" And on he went pointing to each line, "Magnesium, perfect. Creatinine, perfect. Kidney function, perfect. Your liver is *very* clean." Everything was reading in the perfect range. He got to my B12 and Folate levels. I had a gene mutation that required me to take a prescription for both of these. However, I was not allowed to take the medication while undergoing chemo. Consequently, I had been without this much needed prescription strength supplement for seven months. He looked at it and paused, then spoke, "This is interesting, your B12 and Folate look great. What are you doing?" "Nothing!", I exclaimed, "I haven't even taken the prescription for seven months because oncology told me I couldn't take it during chemo." He looked at me in disbelief and said, "Are you serious?? This is unreal!" He continued down the list, in disbelief, showing everything in the normal range.

He got to the thyroid levels and said, "Now your thyroid levels are a little high. We'll need to cut your meds." I've been taking thyroid medications for over 20 years and now, after everything it's just been through, it was functioning better!

He just shook his head in amazement, stopped reading, and as he tapped his fingers on the report, he looked up at us and said, "This is not normal. This is *not* the bloodwork of someone who's just had six months of intense chemo. This is not natural." "You're right! It's supernatural!" I exclaimed. He replied, "I have to concur. I'm going to have a copy of this made for you so you can frame it, because this is definitely an act of God."

He was the same doctor that had started me on thyroid medication over twenty years ago and had monitored it ever since. He also knew all the struggles I had through the years trying to keep my vitamin levels in the healthy range even while taking high quality supplements. I reiterated to him how much energy I had now and that I honestly was feeling better than I'd felt in decades. "Well, your blood work certainly supports that!" He continued, shaking his head in amazement, "I wish I'd have seen you before my last patient. They are a wonderful Christian couple and the husband was just diagnosed with stage four cancer. I would have let you come in to pray for him and his wife!"

I felt like I was floating on air when we walked out of the building. Holding the copy of the results up toward my son, I turned to him with an uncontrollable smile from ear to ear, and exclaimed, *"THESE ARE THE SPOILS OF WAR, BABY!! THIS IS THE EXCEEDINGLY ABUNDANTLY MORE THAN I COULD ASK OR THINK!"*

My family and I had just been through what should have been one of the darkest, scariest years of our lives. But instead, we were able to experience the love, joy, peace, and supernatural healing power of Christ *and* His church!

*"And we know that God causes everything to work together for the good of those who love God and are called according to His purpose for them. For God knew His people in advance, and He chose them to become like*

*His Son, so that His Son would be the firstborn among many brothers and sisters. And having chosen them, He called them to come to Him. And having called them, He gave them right standing with Himself. And having given them right standing, He gave them His glory. What shall we say about such wonderful things as these? If God is for us, who can ever be against us?!"*

*Romans 8:28–31 (NLT)*

So why did I feel so strongly not to do chemo after the first diagnosis only to turn around and agree to it after it recurred six months later? I can only speculate. I just know how strongly I felt about my decisions at each turn. I may never fully understand, but I know if I had done the short sprint of chemo the first time, God may not have been able to accomplish all that He did in all of us during those seven months of such an outpouring of love. I also may not have been able to empathize with those going through such awful circumstances. It really does take a chemo patient to understand what a chemo patient goes through.

Before going through it myself, my mom had gone through it, twice. I thought that I understood (being so close to her). Not the case at all.

At the beginning of November, when finishing up chemo, I had told my family not to expect too much for Christmas this year since I would be too weak to decorate, purchase/wrap gifts, and cook. It turned out just the opposite. Not only did I do all of the above, I even participated in our church's Christmas outreaches to cancer patients and their families, and threw a Christmas party on Christmas Eve! **To God be the glory! Great things He has done!**

## THE AFTER PARTY

Even though my thyroid was better, it was not completely normal yet. The great report, though, encouraged me to keep fighting the good fight, believing God would bring total healing. I felt very strongly compelled by the Holy Spirit to do a 40-day fast after the holidays. I had never gone without food that long, but felt so strongly I was to do it. I didn't want to lose ground or sit back and bask in what God had done. I was hungry for even more. I wanted to experience God in an even deeper, more intimate way. I also felt this journey wasn't yet complete but that the best was still ahead of me. And if a 40-day fast was what it was going to take, I was all in.

During the first three weeks of the fast, I felt something click inside of me as if to say, *"Now, you're free to stop taking all thyroid medication"*. Now, two weeks prior, I had tried to lower it (even further than the doctor had) but within three days, I felt the ill effects. So I immediately went back to the right dose. I thought myself, *"It's okay. I won't be discouraged. I know God will heal me eventually"*. But this time, it wasn't my experimenting, it was a definite *prompting* in my gut saying that it was time. (I had never done anything like this before and am NOT advocating for anyone else to do the same. Serious implications, even death, can occur when tampering with a doctor's prescribed dose. I do not recommend doing this unless given permission by your doctor.)

I stopped the thyroid medications completely. I monitored closely for the slightest ill effects. But none ensued. One week went by; nothing. Two weeks went by; nothing. THREE weeks passed; still nothing. I was healed! Not once have I had one symptom since that day. Three months later I had blood work done which confirmed I was healed. It's now been two years, and my thyroid is still functioning perfectly without medication.

Let me reiterate here the magnitude of this. I could not function without that medication. When my father died in 1997, the stress caused my thyroid to take a serious dive. It was horrific. I immediately gained 35 pounds, went into severe depression and had tightness in my chest. My whole world caved in. I knew I was dying but didn't know why. We were pastoring in California at the time. My husband, quite concerned, called our close friend and doctor from Louisiana. The doctor was so concerned, he bought the first plane ticket out, having me flown directly to him for treatment and told my husband to watch me close until I got on the plane. Just a couple of weeks prior to this, our doctor had a strong, psychologically balanced, male patient, the same age as I was, have the same thing happen to him. In his altered state, the man took a gun and shot himself. Needless to say, for me to have taken this medication for twenty years and now suddenly stop with no detrimental effects is a supernatural miracle, my friends!

## BUT WAIT THERE'S MORE!

Since the chemo, my hips were in a lot of pain and I was still extremely weak. Just walking up the seven steps at work that led to my studio was difficult. I even had to hold on to the rail going down the steps for fear my legs would give out. About 20 days into the fast, the pain in my left hip grew worse and worse. It was radiating up my lower back and down my left leg. After the third day of this, though quite concerned, I went on to bed in a lot of pain. For the first hour in bed, I had to get up to go to the restroom three times. Okay, warning here: This is about to get really gross, but stay with me! Each time I went to the bathroom, I had diarrhea. The third time I went, I passed a large amount of something that was a very bright green. Immediately following that, all the pain in my hip was gone! This fast was detoxing my body! (Stay with me here. I know it's gross but there's an amazing reason for sharing such a private detail!)

The next day, my daughter and three of her friends came home from a trip. When they came in, Lexi (my daughter) asked how I was feeling and how the fast was going. I said, "Well, something pretty amazing happened last night when I went to the restroom, but it's really gross, so I won't tell you…" Well, her friend, Rae, cut me off and excitedly spoke up,"Oh you definitely have to tell us! I totally want to know the details!" (She's in medical school – need I say more?!) They all jumped in with excitement and laughter, "Yes! We want to know!" So, I told them what happened. Rae immediately said, "Oh wow, that's awesome! And it explains so much..". She then proceeded to tell me how her friend had gone through chemo a couple years earlier and was reduced to a wheelchair due to weakness and severe pain in her hips. She said, "...so, that doesn't surprise me at all." A year later, while researching, I came across an article connecting hip pain to toxic build up in the hip area! This 40-day fast was a continued part of my physical healing without me even knowing it at the time. And it was a testimony to these young people of how God leads us by His Holy Spirit and works powerfully in our lives to bring healing.

## ABOVE AND BEYOND BLESSINGS

Along with my continued healing, my family was at the top of my prayer list during this 40-day fast. Our little family had experienced so much hurt, betrayal, and loss in the last 10 years and I was desperate to see God bring total restoration. Within days of beginning the fast, God was moving in a big way. My daughter, who was miserable at her job, suddenly landed a dream job. My son, began getting a rush of new, very high-paying clients in his business. My husband's job was on the line because the owner of the company had recently died and some very wicked and powerful men within the company set their sights on his position and his superior's position. But God gave us a heads-up at every turn. He exposed to us the enemy's schemes in a dream, continued to give us insight before these men attempted their antics and gave Jonathan wisdom and protection at every turn.

The time spent in prayer during the fast was so glorious that I caught a glimpse of what Jesus meant when He told His disciples, "...*I have food to eat you know nothing of...*" (John 4:32). My appetite had been replaced with an insatiable hunger for the presence of God! It had long grieved my heart that, after the devastating hurt, my daughter and husband were no longer "...*planted in the house of the Lord…"* (Psalm 92:13). They only attended on Sunday mornings. During the fast, my husband felt compelled to start a men's bible study. Together, we started having regular prayer gatherings in our home and our daughter decided she wanted to join the worship team at church!

Almost daily, God was opening doors for me to minister. I was accepting invitations to speak about my experience and God kept bringing women to me to pray with, counsel, and minister to in incredible ways. And…I penned the majority of this book during that fast!

What Jesus has done, is doing, and will do in my future has me in awe of Him. Even during the entire Job-like experience we went through the last ten years, His goodness truly is *"… the same yesterday, today and forever"* (Hebrews 13:8). My next book will probably be about those years and the miraculous way God *"…kept us alive in [our] time of famine…"* (Psalm 33:18–19) and held us close through that dark valley. Or maybe it will be about the incredible miracles we experienced and witnessed while ministering in a town in the Napa Valley that was riddled with cults and demonic activity. We have experienced countless miracles through the years as we have walked daily in Christ. There is NEVER a dull moment when our hearts and lives are completely committed and surrendered to Him. Neither should there be *any* fear for He will *never* leave us or forsake us. Life in Christ is *the* ultimate adventure!

## PRAYER

"Heavenly Father, thank you that I can come to You in my hour of need. You extended the invitation, "Come to me all who are weary and heavy laden" (Matt. 11:28). You are there with arms open wide to embrace me and give me rest! I rest in Your presence; in Your strong arms. Help me, Father, to meditate on Your promises day and night. Empower me to "abide" in Christ daily and to "pray without ceasing". I lay down every sin at your feet. Forgive me and wash me clean. I receive forgiveness from You and I extend it to those who have hurt me. Strengthen my faith, Lord, as I meditate on Your Word. I believe You are the Healer. Show me what Your will for me is in this trial. Whether it's to live for Your glory or die for Your glory, either way, I win because I have You as my Lord, my Savior, my God. I want You to be honored in my words and my actions. I trust You and I stand firm on the scriptures YOU give to ME. I love You, Lord! I pray this in the name of Jesus, Jehovah Rapha, my Healer. Amen."

## FOR REFLECTION AND MEDITATION

### MEMORIZE Proverbs 4:20-22 NASB

*"My son (daughter), give attention to My Words, incline your ears to My sayings. Do not let them depart from your eyes; keep them in the midst of your heart; for they are life to those who find them and health to all their flesh." ["daughter" added]*

### DECIDE What You Believe

*Do I believe in God? Do I believe the Bible is the inspired Word of God? Do I believe the Holy Spirit, through the Word, will guide me into all truth concerning my circumstances?*

*Write down the scriptures God impresses on your heart as you read them.*

## DON'T GO IT ALONE

*We need other believers. And they need you! Be transparent and humble. Share the Word together (attend a Bible study or start your own in your neighborhood). Pray together. Pray, pray, pray with others and alone. Sing praises to the Lord EVERYDAY. He inhabits your praise! (Ps.23:3)*

*Notes*

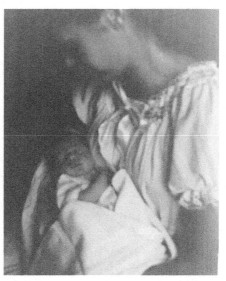

*Harold and Saundra (my parents)*    *My mother and me*

*My sister, Terri, and me*

*Terri and me. Before my healing, I was usually too sick to play outside. My big sister would help me so I could go outside and "play."*

*The day we left Portland. Family photo after church with my mother's parents, brother and sister-in-law. I was so sick, and in so much pain from the shot I had the day before, I could barely stand.*

*My father and I on the 700 Club with Ben Kinchlow, circa 1982. We held hands at the end of the interview and prayed for the viewers around the world to personally experience the healing power of Jesus Christ.*

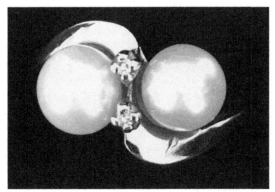

*The pearl ring given to my mother after my healing in 1966.*

*The most amazing man I know. My rock. He is grace and strength personified.*

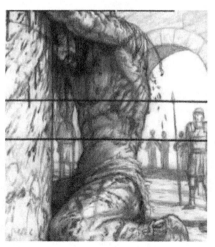

*This is the picture that I would look at to remind me of the price that Jesus paid for my healing. I refused to let His suffering be in vain. (Artist unknown)*

*Chapter Six*

# POWERFUL PRAYERS

*"... The earnest prayer of a righteous person has great power and produces wonderful results."*

*James 5:16 (NLT)*

*If you abide in Me, and My words abide in you, you will ask what you desire, and it shall be done for you. By this is My Father glorified, that you bear much fruit; and so prove to be My disciples"*

*John 15:7–8 (NHEB)*

## DEFINING PRAYER

COUNTLESS VOLUMES OF books have been written on prayer, yet I have found that a vast number of religious people know very little about what the Bible actually says about prayer. Is prayer just a memorized recital handed down from generation to generation like the rosary, for example? Is prayer mere conversation with God? Is prayer just laying out all of our wants, needs, and desires to the air and hoping a mysterious god hears, cares, and at best, answers? How do we even know if and when God hears our prayers? Other than their limited knowledge of The Lord's Prayer, many base their

beliefs about prayer on hearsay and assumptions, then wonder why
their prayers seem empty and futile; or at best, minimally answered.
Because this is a chapter *of* prayers and not a chapter *about* prayer, I
won't elaborate too much on the topic. However, I feel it is imperative that we understand what prayer really is and what the Bible sets
as a prerequisite to God's hearing and answering of our prayers. See
the suggested reading in the back of this book for excellent books
on prayer. The men and women who wrote these books have supernatural insight into powerful prayer. They have helped me tremen-
dously through the years when I wanted to go deeper in my inter-
cessory prayer and intimate communion with Christ through prayer.

In my experience throughout decades of ministry, I realize that
few Christians even know that, according to Scripture, there are
certain situations where God chooses not to even hear our prayers
(see chapter 4). That's right, God actually chooses to turn a deaf
ear to certain prayers. I don't know about you, but that's a very
scary thought to most of us. The only time most people even pray is
when they have a need. How frightening to think that, in our time
of need, we can pray until we're blue in the face, and God will not
even hear us (1 Samuel 15:23; Isaiah 59:2; Psalm 66:18; Proverbs
28:9). Maybe that's one answer to the question so many ask, "If God
is love, why...?" You can fill in the rest as we all have heard it and
even said it ourselves at one time or another. Is it God's fault that
people suffer and prayers go unanswered? There is one very simple answer to that question: *No.* Every good and perfect gift comes
from the Father above. Addictions, adultery, and all sexual immorality, disease, abuse, greed, selfishness, murder... all stem from the
wicked heart of fallen mankind. Jesus came to redeem the heart of
man from its wickedness. He showed us His will at Calvary, that all
should be free from sin and death to walk in intimacy with God. It
is His desire that every human possesses the kind of love for others
that honors God and honors others over their own selfishness. The
Apostle Paul put it like this:

*"Love must be sincere. Detest what is evil; cling to what is good. Be devoted*
*to one another in brotherly love. Outdo yourselves*
*in honoring one another."*

*Romans 12:9–10 (Berean Study Bible)*

Then there's the other question so many ask: "If God is love, why does He allow this to happen to me?" I personally feel that question would be better asked like this: "If God is love, why does He allow someone as selfish as I, to breathe another breath?" It's so easy to want to question why God doesn't strike the mean dictator dead and cause steak and lobster to rain down on all the starving children of Africa while we live in denial that perhaps we are just as much a part of the problem as "the man", or the Church, or our neighbor, or ISIS, or…or… Very seldom do any of us own up to the realization that perhaps we are personally part of the problem.

The pharisees in Jesus' day are a prime example. They did everything right. They were more law abiding than anyone. They gave to the poor, obeyed the Ten Commandments, lived clean lives, and were the example of model citizens. Yet Jesus referred to them as white-washed tombs. They were beautifully painted with good works but their hearts were black and dead. They were so righteous in their own eyes and yet so spiritually blind that they could not even recognize the Messiah when they were staring Him in the face. They were the very ones that turned Jesus over to be crucified. Jesus had the ability to look past their shiny veneer, just like He does ours today, and see just how hollow our goodness is.

Now before you start pointing your finger at the religious leaders, past or present, as the sole problem, remember that Scripture says the mob, or crowds of people, turned against Jesus and shouted for Him to be crucified. Even worse, His beloved disciples that lived with Him for three years, scampered like scared rabbits when push came to shove. So let's just bring this home and keep it real. God's not impressed with how many times we go to church, teach a Sunday

School class, feed the poor, jog for charity, and say our memorized prayers. Nope. Not impressed at all.

So what does impress God? His Son, Jesus. And a humble heart after God that embraces Jesus as Lord and Savior. That's it. A heart that is humble, teachable, ready and willing to answer His call to walk intimately with Him. A heart that longs to know Him more than anything or anyone else. A person who desires and chooses to live and move and have their being in constant intimacy with Him. Because from that, God can do immeasurably more in us and in the lives around us than we could ask or think. Good works don't save people. Jesus does. Good works don't make us righteous. Jesus does. That's the power of the message of the thief on the cross next to Jesus. He never had a chance to do good works or memorize and recite the right prayers. But he reached out to Jesus from a humble heart that acknowledged Jesus was the Son of God and asked Jesus to let him be a part of His kingdom. Jesus was quick to respond to his prayer and to receive him.

Don't misunderstand me. I'm not dismissing the importance of good works. Good deeds should be a natural outflow of a heart surrendered to Christ. But without Christ at the helm, it's the heart of every person that will ultimately manifest into *selfish* actions.

We must stop believing the lie that we are good. We are not good. Only Christ in us, the hope of glory, is good. Jeremiah (17:9) tells us that *"The human heart is the most deceitful of all things, and desperately wicked. Who really knows how bad it is?"* We have innately wicked, selfish, and pathetic hearts in need of a Savior who can take our wicked hearts and create in us a heart like His.

*".. out of a person's heart come evil thoughts, sexual immorality, theft, murder, adultery, greed, wickedness, deceit, lustful desires, envy, slander, pride, and foolishness. All these vile things come from within; they are what defile you."*

*Mark 7:20–23 (NLT)*

So how do we achieve a life that pleases God? Jesus answers that question:

*"Then Jesus said to His disciples, 'Whoever wants to be My disciple must deny themselves and take up their cross and follow Me.'"*
*Matthew 16:24 (NIV)*

When Jesus said we must take up our cross, He didn't mean a literal cross, but what the cross represents: a crucifixion of our "flesh", or our own will of "self", in order to follow Him. Jesus modeled for us how we are to live our lives. He explained how He lived His life:

*"...I tell you the truth, the Son can do nothing by Himself. He does only What He sees the Father doing. Whatever the Father does, the Son also does."*
*John 5:19 (NLT)*

He told His disciples,

*"I am in the Father, and you are in Me, and I am in you. Whoever has My commands and keeps them is the one who loves Me. The one who loves Me will be loved by My Father, and I too will love them and show Myself to them."*
*John 14:20 (NIV)*

That is a beautiful depiction of intimacy with God; when we are so in love with Jesus that we desire to do nothing apart from Him. Just as He did nothing apart from what His Father led Him to do, so we are to live the same.

A follower of Christ is not someone who 'lives on the edge' of holiness. Those who have truly surrendered their hearts and lives to Christ do not try to twist scripture to suit their lifestyle of sin, because their delight is not in their sin, it's in Christ. A true disciple of Christ will go the extra mile... all the way to the cross, to abide in the fullness of Christ, not the fullness of their sin.

Those who belong to Christ Jesus have crucified the flesh with its passions and desires (Galatians 5:24). God's grace is not a license to sin, it's the power to be set free from sin.

When we are truly in love with Christ, we no longer live as slaves to our own lust and ever-increasing wickedness but we now offer ourselves as 'slaves to righteousness' so that we may become in holy unity with Him as He is in holy unity with the Father. Remember, holiness/purity is the antithesis of sin, which is impurity.

Unfortunately, 'holiness' is taboo in most Christian circles today. We live in a "whatever is truth to you" generation that does not want to hear about spiritual disciplines, a standard of holiness, or living a lifestyle that may be contrary to personal choice. But God made it very clear that those who are not holy will not see the Lord (Hebrews 12:14). Do you have a sacred confidence you will see Him when He returns for His bride, the Church? Do you need to see God in your life? Your circumstances? Matthew 5:8 says it is the pure in heart who will see God.

I want, with everything in me, to see God move in my life. I believe you do too. That is the reason you are reading this book. However, we must be intellectually honest with ourselves. We cannot willfully hold onto the sin and compromise in our lives and expect God to be a part of it. He will not and He cannot. He is Holy. It is who He is.

Furthermore, the Kingdom of God is not a democracy. Your opinion is of no consequence to the edict of a king. We can twist Scripture all we want in order to condone our sin, but when we stand before the great Judge, it is Truth (not our opinion of it) that will reign supreme.

## PRAYER IS PERSONAL AND INTIMATE CONVERSATION

With everything in me, I want you to experience the exhilarating power, authority, joy, peace, and freedom of an intimate prayer life with God. I love the Scripture, where Jesus, speaking to the church says, *"Here I am! I stand at the door and knock. If anyone hears My voice and opens the door, I will come in and eat with that person, and they with Me"* (Revelation 3:20). He's speaking here of a very personal, private fellowship. In the Jewish culture of that day, to sit down and share a meal with someone in your home was considered a very sacred, intimate practice of fellowship. It was not proper to eat with someone that was not of the Jewish faith. Sitting down for a meal together was considered an intimate time of communion in their culture; a time for engaging in personal, private conversations. The kind of conversation you would have with your spouse, best friend, parent, or child. Not the kind of conversation you engage in while having lunch with co-workers or acquaintances.

He doesn't want you coming to Him merely reciting memorized prayers like a robot. In essence, Jesus is saying, in this passage, *"I want to come into your inner life—your heart. That place no one else abides but you, and commune with you about every intimate detail of your life as you share them* with Me and I share My love, wisdom, power, peace, all that I am with you". Talk about the ultimate friend! Jesus Christ, the Son of the living God, knocking at the door of your heart and asking to come in—it doesn't it get any better than that!

Talk with Him today. Tell Him everything that is in your heart and on your mind. Lay your hurts, desires, concerns, everything out before Him. He wants to hear it all. Not in a whiny complaining sort of way. Remember who you are talking to and do so with respect and honor in humility. Do so by faith, knowing that He not only wants to hear it, He wants to move on your behalf in all of those things.

Remember who you are in Christ: a child of the most high God. You are royalty, so approach Him in a manner worthy of your calling. And don't forget to love Him, worship Him, praise Him, sing songs to Him, whatever is in your heart—show Him your love and gratitude. He is the Lover of your soul. Let His love wash over you, bringing healing where there is hurt, loneliness, emptiness.

## PRAYER IS WAGING WAR: MAKE SURE YOU ARE ARMED FOR BATTLE

Whether praying for healing or anything else, I love to quote His Word in my prayers. Prayer is warfare. And though we live in this world, we do not wage war as the world does. According to 2 Corinthians 10:3–4, the weapons we wage war with are not the weapons of the world. On the contrary, they have divine power that demolishes spiritual strongholds.

*"We wrestle not against flesh and blood, but against principalities, against powers, against the rulers of darkness of this world, against spiritual wickedness in high places."*

*Ephesians 6:12(KJV)*

To fight a spiritual enemy requires spiritual weapons. And the Word of God is our most powerful weapon. God places His Word even above His name (Psalm 138:2). When we are instructed to put on the full armor of God to fight our battles, the only weapon mentioned is *"the sword of the spirit, which is the Word of God"* (Eph. 6:17).

*"Therefore put on the full armor of God, so that when the day of evil comes, you may be able to stand your ground, and after you have done everything, to stand. Stand firm then with the belt of Truth buckled around your waist, with the breastplate of righteousness in place, and with your feet fitted with the readiness that comes from the gospel of peace. In addition to all this, take up the shield of faith, with which you can extinguish all the flaming arrows of the evil one. Take the helmet of salvation and the sword of the Spirit, which is the Word of God. And pray in the Spirit in all occasions with all kinds of prayers and requests. With this in mind, be alert and always keep on praying for all the Lord's people. Pray also for me, that whenever I speak, words may be given me so that I will fearlessly make known the mystery of the gospel."*

*Ephesians 6:13–19(NIV)*

The Word of God is the only offensive weapon mentioned in this passage. Every other piece of armor is for defense. If we are going on the offense in prayer, we need to pull out our sword of the Spirit, the Word, and fight the enemy in faith. It's one thing to pray my words (and I do it everyday) but it's "a whole 'nother level" when I begin wielding the Word of God from my lips. If *"the power of life and death are in the tongue"* (Prov. 18:21), how much more power flows from the lips of the one speaking by faith the very Word of God over his circumstances!

This is how Jesus Christ Himself defeated Satan in the wilderness (when Satan came to tempt Jesus at the end of His 40-day fast). Every temptation Satan hurled at Him, Jesus resisted by quoting Scripture (Matt.4:1–11). Scripture is your weapon against all the attacks of the enemy!

## PRAYING IN THE NAME OF JESUS

If you feel you are under attack, and can't recall a single scripture, call on the name of Jesus! Romans 10:13 tells us that all who call on the name of Jesus will be saved. Remember, Jesus is the Word (John 1:1). There have been many times in my life when the only prayer I could say is *"Jesus!"* in a moment of emergency and desperation.

Ben, a real estate agent and personal friend of ours, went to a resort near the church we were pastoring in Napa Valley. He was going to view the property as the listing agent. This was a New Age occultic resort where the guru led people in practices such as transcendental meditation and astral projection.

While touring the property with a member of the property's staff, they came across a room of people sitting silently on the floor in a meditation pose. The staff member would not permit Ben to enter the room as he proceeded to tell Ben that the people in the room had left their bodies (astral projection). As he peered through the window in the door, Ben joked with the guy and said, "Hey, why don't we hide their bodies and then when they try to come back, they won't be able to find themselves!" Needless to say, the man didn't appreciate Ben's humor.

Ben continued, "Seriously though, what if they leave their body and they fly around and get lost? What then? Have you ever had someone not make it back to their body?" The man replied, "You can't get lost. But we always give every participant specific instructions what to do should they encounter a dark spirit. If you come across the dark spirit, the only way you can get away from it is to say the name '*Jesus*'". "Jesus (Christ)" is the most powerful name in all the universe." Ben looked at the man in amazement and asked, "Well, if you know that, why won't you make Jesus the Lord and Savior of your life!?" The man retorted sharply, "No. We won't do that. We don't believe that way." They preferred to be their own god (the basis of the New Age religion).

They wouldn't serve Jesus as their Lord and Savior but would use His name. What a sacrilegious, profane misuse of His holy name for the purpose of perverted, self-serving intimidation! This reminds me of the Scripture, Matthew 7:22 that says, *"Many will say to me in that day, 'Lord, Lord, have we not prophesied in Thy name? and **in Thy name have cast out devils?** and in Thy name done many wonderful works?' And then will I profess unto them, I never knew you: depart from me, ye that work iniquity."*

We are called to live with a reverent, holy, passionate love for His name. God's name represents His holy character and His nature. His name tells us what kind of God He is. There are over 300 names attributed to God in the Bible and each is a revelation of His holy, sacred character. Never are they to be uttered or treated lightly. The name of God was so profoundly sacred that the orthodox Jews would not pronounce the name of God in normal conversation. In fact, as the scribes were making copies of the Holy Scripture, when they came to the name of God they would place their pen down, rise, bathe themselves, and put on different garments. Then they would write with a pen that had never been used before the holy name of God. It was considered that holy. It *is* that holy, that sacred, that reverenced, and that honored in all the universe.

*"Salvation is found in no one else, for there is no other name under heaven given to mankind by which we must be saved."*

*Acts 4:12 (Romans 10:13)*

The name of Jesus is the most powerful name in all the universe for all of time and eternity! Satan must bow to the name of Jesus. Demons must bow to the name of Jesus. There is absolutely, unequivocally, no power that can stand against the name of Jesus Christ. The Salvation of man comes in the name of Jesus (Acts 4:12). The Devil is powerless because of the name of Jesus (Luke 10:17). Demons are cast out in the name of Jesus (Mark 16:17–18). Healing occurs in the name of Jesus (Acts 3:6; 3:16; 4:10). We are baptized into a glorious new life in the name of Jesus (Matthew 28:19). We are justified in the name of Jesus (1 Cor. 6:11). As believers, everything we say and do is to be done in His name (Col. 3:17).

*"Therefore God exalted Him to the highest place and gave Him the Name that is above every name, that at the name of Jesus every knee should bow, in heaven and on earth and under the earth, and every tongue acknowledge that Jesus Christ is Lord, to the glory of God the Father."*

*Philippians 2:9–11 (NIV)*

Some of the most powerful passages in all of Scripture are the very words of Jesus Christ, found in the book of John:

*"Verily, Verily I say unto you, he that believeth on Me, the works that I do shall he do also; and greater works than these shall he do ... whatsoever ye shall ask in my name, that will I do, that the Father may be glorified in the Son. If ye shall ask anything in My name, I will do it ... "*

*John 14:12–14 (KJV)*

Jesus speaking to His disciples, said:

*"...verily, verily I say unto you, Whatsoever ye shall ask the Father **in My name**, He will give it you."*
*John 16:23(KJV)*

It is critical to your faith that you grasp the truth about the power of the Word of God and the name of Jesus in defeating your enemy. When we come to the powerful knowledge of *Who* the Word is, coupled with the power of understanding our identity in Jesus Christ, we can do great exploits to the glory of God.

## AUTHORITY OVER DEMONIC POWERS

When I was a young girl, around 10 years old, a woman showed up at our church during a Wednesday evening service. Unbeknownst to us, she was in the occult and came to the church that night for the sole purpose of killing my father (the pastor) and burning the church to the ground. While sitting in the service, waiting for the opportune moment to make her move, God made His move instead. While my father was giving an invitation for people to come down to the altar to receive Christ, she "saw" her mother (who had been dead for years) standing at the altar. She got out of her seat and proceeded to walk down the aisle to her mother. She knew it would also be her chance to get to the preacher to kill him. When she arrived at the altar, her mother was no longer there but suddenly she looked up and saw the cross on the wall over the baptistery. According to her testimony, she said the cross illuminated, came off the wall and came toward her. It was getting smaller and brighter as it got closer to her. When it reached her, it touched her forehead and she immediately fell to the ground and experienced a supernatural revelation of Jesus Christ. She told us when the cross touched her forehead, a power shot through her like she had never experienced. It was a love she could not even explain. She went to the ground a satanist but came up a born-again believer in Christ!

A few weeks after her miraculous conversion, she called our home in the middle of the night quite distraught. When my father answered the phone, he heard her say, in a frantic whisper, *"Pastor! What do I do?! Anton LaVay just appeared at the end of my bed and is telling me I must renounce Christ and return to the Satanist church!"* My father told her, *"Evelyn, that is a demon. You have authority over it as a child of God. Point at it and tell it, 'Leave now in the name of Jesus and never return'"*. She did what my father said, and immediately it disappeared never to return again.

I learned a lot about the power of God and the power of the enemy through watching this woman's life and hearing her testimonies through the years. It also showed me how clueless people are to the very real enemy of our lives, how very deceptive he is, and how powerless he is when we walk in our identity and exercise our authority as children of the most high God. It also strengthened my confidence as a believer in Christ. As Galatians 2:20 and Luke 10:19 tell us:

*"I have been crucified with Christ;* **it is no longer I who live, but Christ lives in me***: and* **the life which I now live** *in the flesh* **I live by faith in the Son of God***, who loved me and gave Himself for me."*
*Galatians 2:20 (NKJV)*

*Jesus said to His disciples (that includes all believers),*
*"I watched Satan fall from heaven like [a flash of] lightning.* **Listen carefully: I have given you authority** *[that you now possess] to tread on serpents and scorpions, and [the ability to exercise authority]* **over all the power of the enemy** *(Satan); and nothing will [in any way] harm you."*
*Luke 10:18b–19 (AMP)*

We have nothing to fear when we are hidden in Christ. Satan was defeated once and for all when Christ was crucified and rose again. He is powerless—defeated by the power of Christ Jesus. For those who are in Christ, nothing the enemy brings against us can prevail unless we choose to let it. Satan is a liar (the "father of lies") and a constant accuser of those who are believers in Christ. Why is that? Because he has no real power over us. He must, like he did with Adam and Eve, convince us of a lie so we will be tempted to not only walk away from God's power-packed truths but embrace the lie. Then he can take us captive. But when we call on Jesus with repentant hearts, we are set free from our sin and its strongholds. It's important to remember though, what Jesus said in verse 20 of that same passage in Luke:

*"Nevertheless do not rejoice at this, that the spirits are subject to you, but rejoice that your names are recorded in heaven."*
*Luke 10:20 (AMP)*

## PRAYING THE WORD OF GOD

This proved to be my most powerful weapon during my battle with cancer. While in prayer, I found that when I began praying scripture over my body and my circumstances, the power of my prayers catapulted to another level of power. Praying, meditating, memorizing, and declaring scripture were a continual part of every day *and* night during this season like never before. I obviously knew cancer would be a challenge physically but I didn't expect the cancer to be such a mental and spiritual battle—an *intense* mental and spiritual battle! As I mentioned in previous chapters, I kept the Word with me at *all* times; even playing audio of it when I didn't have the strength to read, I can't encourage you enough to memorize scripture and pray God's Word. It is alive and active, powerful and able to do great exploits. And it will not return void (Isaiah 55:11). Note how much scripture is contained in the prayers in this chapter. If you do not have those scriptures memorized, pick one today to start memorizing. Never stop memorizing verses that empower your walk with the Lord.

## PRAYING THE LORD'S PRAYER

When you don't know where to begin, 'The Lord's Prayer' is a great place to start. Jesus gave us this model prayer in Matthew 6:9–13 and Luke 11:1–4:

*"Our Father which art in heaven, Hallowed be Thy name.*
*Thy Kingdom come, Thy will be done, in earth, as it is in heaven. Give us*
*this day our daily bread. And forgive us our debts, as we forgive our debtors.*
*And lead us not into temptation; but deliver us from evil: For Thine is the*
*kingdom, and the power, and the glory, for ever. Amen."*
*Matthew 6:9–13 (KJV)*

I use this prayer all the time as a model, or framework, for my personal prayer. I don't just pray this for me but also for my husband, my children, those in authority over me (ministers, bosses, teachers, government leaders, law enforcement, and emergency responders, etc), or specific people or situations that are on my heart. Basically, it is the outline, or skeleton, that I build my prayer upon.

What really started me on this great way of utilizing the Lord's Prayer as an outline (or basis) for praying, was when I was asked to pray at a large city-wide ecumenical event many years ago. There were going to be people from quite a diversity of denominational backgrounds at this religious gathering as well as many top government officials. I wanted to pray sincerely and uncompromisingly from my heart yet without bringing unnecessary offense to anyone in attendance (and thus negate the intention of the meeting). Most importantly, I wanted to pray in a way that *God* would have me pray. But I was at a loss how to pray *for* this meeting, much less *at* the meeting. While in my personal prayer time I started to pray about the upcoming meeting. I remember saying, *"Lord, I don't even know how to pray for a meeting like this. Please show me how to pray for this."* Immediately, I recalled the disciples asking Jesus how to pray (Luke 11:1–13). "That's it!" I thought. How obvious! Just pray how He told all the disciples to pray! So I began praying for the event using The Lord's Prayer as a guide. It ended up being an incredibly powerful time of prayer. I was able to pray effectively when I initially had no clue how to even begin. As I implemented this method in my prayer the day of the city-wide event, the power of God came down upon that meeting that day and we were all profoundly impacted by the power of God made manifest. I have since used this model to pray often about anything and everything.

## TIME TO PRAY

Enough *about* prayer. It's time to pray! What a privilege to talk with God! The following are prayers that I have prayed. They come from my heart. Don't feel that I have cornered the market with these prayers and that by memorizing and reciting them, you'll suddenly be praying right. These are merely to help you pray from *your* heart. I have a lot of books on prayer. During my chemotherapy, I referred to one or two of those books more than once to help me pray when I couldn't even think straight to pray as my heart desired. That is what I hope these prayers will do for you; help you on your journey.

## MODELING THE LORD'S PRAYER

Many know the Lord's Prayer from memory. If you do not, I encourage you to commit it to memory so you can refer to it as you pray. The following is a prayer I prayed using the Lord's Prayer as my guide.

*"Heavenly Father, You reign from Your throne in heaven. Holy is Your name. You are MY Father! I love You and praise You and thank You for all You've done for me! Your name is above all names. There is none like You—not in heaven or earth or below the earth. You are good and perfect in every way. You are the Alpha, the Omega, the beginning and the end. You are the Omniscient, Omnipotent, triumphant King of Kings and Lord of Lords and I give You this day, the honor due Your name. You are the Great I Am. Everything I will ever need is found in You. I love You and thank You that I can call on Your name, LORD, and be saved. I*

*thank You for the blood of Jesus that washes my heart clean so that I may come boldly before Your throne. I bow my heart before You. Let Your kingdom come and Your will be done in my life today, as it is in heaven. Empower me to live this day for You. May Your kingdom reign in my heart and life today and empower me to do Your will, not mine. I set my mind on the truths of Your Word today, not mine or other's. Help me to have a teachable heart that is pliable in Your hands, oh God. Please give me today all that I need physically and spiritually to thrive for Your glory and to be all You purposed me to be. Search my heart, oh God, and show me anything that is not pleasing to You. [Wait for Him to show you before proceeding.] Please forgive me of _____ (naming specific sins that come to mind). Wash me clean by Your blood. Empower me this day, to walk in Your victory over _____(name the sin). Help me to "keep my mind stayed on You" (Isaiah 26:3) and not to think about sinful things. Thank You that "Your mercies are new every morning" (Lam.3:22–23). Because You have forgiven me of so much, I forgive all those who have sinned against me or are indebted to me in any way. I choose today to forgive _____(name them by name). Lead me not into temptation today but help me to walk in victory. Give me Your wisdom and power to avoid temptation and to walk on the paths of righteousness for Your name's sake. Please protect me and deliver me from evil. Surround me with Your angels and shield me from the enemy. For Yours is the kingdom and power and glory. I can do nothing apart from You, but am more than a conqueror in Christ Jesus. I give You the glory for everything. You are worthy of my praise and I praise You with my whole heart today. In Jesus' name I pray. Amen."*

## PRAYERS FOR HEALING AND DELIVERANCE

*"Father I thank You that in the beginning was the Word. And the Word was with God and the Word was God. And the Word became flesh and dwelt among us. (John 1) That flesh was wounded for my transgressions, bruised for my iniquities. The chastisement for my peace was upon Him and by His stripes I am healed. (Isaiah 53:5). My Savior was tortured and beaten beyond recognition so that I might be healed and I refuse to let that be in vain.*

*You said in 2 Corinthians 1:20 that every promise in the book is yes and amen for those who are in Christ Jesus and because I have given my heart and life to You, those promises are mine. I am more than a conqueror in Christ Jesus (Romans 8:37). You sent Your Word and healed me, and delivered me from all my destructions (Psalm 107:20). I bind this (name the disease/affliction/addiction)_____ in the name of Jesus and command it to be gone from my body. I will not die but live and declare the works of the Lord (Ps.118:17) because You forgive all my iniquities, You deliver my life from destruction, You heal all my diseases, You restore my life and heal me of my wounds (Ps.103). I am more than a conqueror in Christ Jesus. The curse of sin and death is broken and the Spirit of the Living God dwells mightily within me (Gal.3:13). And where the Spirit of the Lord is there is life and liberty. Jesus bore the curse for me, therefore, I forbid_____ to inhabit and dwell in my body. Your Word is alive and active and the power of life and death are in the spoken word (Hebrews 4:12; Proverbs 18:21). Therefore, I speak Your Word, oh God, over my body with the authority You have given me in the name of Jesus (Mark 16:17). You, oh Lord, are my strength and my stronghold; and my refuge in the day of affliction. You rescue me from every trap and protect me from deadly disease (Jeremiah 16:19; Psalm 27:1; Ps.91:2). I bless Your holy name and I forget not all Your benefits (Psalm 105)! I hold fast to the confession of my faith without wavering, for You who promised is faithful (Hebrews 10:23)! All glory, honor and praise to God the Father, Christ the Son, and the Holy Spirit who comforts and empowers me. In Jesus' name I pray. Amen."*

## HEALING/DELIVERANCE

*"Heavenly Father, I look to You to meet me at my point of need, for You are the only One who can work the impossible in my heart, mind, and body. You admonished me to come to You and cast all my cares at Your feet because You care for me (1 Peter 5:7). So I come before You now to ask You to move in power in my weakness. Set me free from _____ that so easily grabs ahold of me and leads me into a place of defeat and desolation. I surrender my thoughts and my will to Yours. Help me, Lord, as I resist the devil and the temptations and lies he hurls at me today (James 4:7). I ask for the wisdom and discernment not only to recognize the bait of Satan for what it is, but also to recognize the way of escape You have set before me (1 Corinthians 10:13). Fill me today with Your*

*Holy Spirit, I pray (Ephesians 5:18). Come, Holy Spirit, I need you. I want you. I can't even die to 'self' without Your empowering me. Victory does not come from my own strength but by Your Spirit (Zechariah 4:6). Help me to keep my focus on You and the truths of Your Word today (Is.26:3). I put on the armor of God, take my position in this battle, worship You, and trust You to fight for me and to bring me to victory (Ephesians 6:10–18; 2 Chronicles 20:17). Thank You in advance for the victory! Thank You that no weapon formed against me will prosper (Isaiah 54:17)! Thank You that You never leave me nor forsake me (Hebrews 13:5)! Thank You that You reward me with victory and breakthrough when I diligently seek You (Hebrews 11:6). I will seek diligently after You when it comes to walking in victory over _____ today. I will diligently worship and praise You throughout the day, taking time to stop and tell You I love You and am so grateful for Your presence in my heart and life (Psalm 34)! Thank You for Your presence in my life today (Psalm 46:1)! I refuse to believe the lies of my flesh, the world, and the devil. I combat those lies with Your Word and declare that today, victory is mine in Christ Jesus. Amen."*

## HOLDING FAST AND STANDING FIRM AGAINST RETALIATION

About three months after receiving the good news that I was cancer-free, I had a vividly detailed dream that I was at the hospital and found out the cancer was back with a vengeance and they just sent me home to die. In the dream, the cancer was so bad the doctor couldn't even tell me to my face. It was a huge, gangrenous thing spread over half my leg and they said it would just take over my body and I would die this horrific death because of it. Dreams can seem so real sometimes and this was one of those times. I woke up dazed and thought, "What was that!? Is it true!?" When I finally got my bearing and realized it was just a dream, I knew I had to combat it with Scripture. (Remember: the Word of God is alive and active and sharper than any two-edged sword and the power of life and death are in the tongue!) So I did. I began the following prayer by thanking the Lord out loud for my healing.

*"Thank You, Lord that You healed me! Thank You that it will not come back on me and that no weapon formed against me shall prosper (Nahum 1:6; Isaiah 54:17). I thank You that it is finished. By Your stripes I am healed (Isaiah 53:5). You sent Your Word and healed me (Psalm 107:20). I will not die, but live and declare the works of the Lord (Psalm 118:17). When the enemy comes in like a flood, YOU, oh LORD, raise up a standard against it (Isaiah 59:19). Thank You that I overcame cancer by the blood of the Lamb and the word of my testimony (Revelation 12:11). I bless You Lord, with everything in me and I forget not all Your benefits: You forgave my sins, HEALED ALL MY DIS-EASES, REDEEMED MY LIFE FROM DESTRUCTION, crown me with lovingkindness and tender mercies, and those mercies are new this morning, and You satisfy my mouth with good things and restore the strength of my youth as the eagles (Psalm 103:1–5)! You have given me power over all the power of the enemy (Luke 10:19). I resist the lies and attack of the enemy and he must flee in Jesus' name (James 4:7)! The Spirit of Life, The Living God, dwells mightily within me (Colossians 1:29) so I command every cell and system in my body right now to line up with the power of the Spirit of the Living God in me (John 14:13). I command you to function in perfect health and strength. I command any and every death giving cell in my body to die and be purged from my body now, in Jesus' name. My body, mind, and spirit will live and declare the works of the Lord, today! The devil is a liar and an accuser of the brethren but greater is He that is in me (John 8:44; Rev. 12:10; 1 John 4:4)! The Word of God dwells richly in me and You, oh Lord, watch over Your Word to perform it. It will NOT return void (Jer.1:12; Is.55:11). Thank You, Heavenly Father, for all You are and all You've done in my life! And I thank You that You will satisfy me with long life (Ps.91:16). Praise and glory and honor be to Your name!"*

I continued to worship and praise the Lord (turning on worship music and singing loudly for all of Heaven and Hell to hear!). When I checked my Facebook later that day, I was once again reminded how cool God is—how He went before me to remind me to stand firm in what I know to be true. This is the scripture He gave me the day before the awful dream, and I had posted it on Facebook to share with everyone:

*"In the morning, as they went along, they saw the fig tree withered from the roots. Peter remembered and said to Jesus, "Rabbi, look! The fig tree you cursed has withered!" "HAVE FAITH IN GOD" Jesus answered. "Stand firm in your belief of what has already been done."*

*Mark 11:20–22*

God is so awesome! He is so faithful! He was already in my tomorrow and was once again preparing me ahead of time for the enemy's attack. His goodness and mercy follow us ALL the days of our lives. He gives us reminders in the morning of His brand new mercies so we can live and declare the works of the LORD. JESUS is THE NAME above cancer and *any* weapon of the enemy formed against those who are in Christ Jesus! Whether in life or in death, we win! Healing and victory is ours either way. Nothing can take our salvation or our joy unless we willingly surrender it. Take your position in this battle and stand firm, my fellow soldier. We are on the winning side. No sickness. No addiction. No failure. (Though we fall, we get right back up and walk in His love and mercy [Proverbs 24:16; 1 John 1:9].) Nothing can defeat us when we are hidden in Christ Jesus, filled with the Holy Spirit and armed with the undefeatable, living Word of God! His NAME is VICTORY! And He has given us His Name! If you have surrendered your heart and life to Jesus and made Him your Lord and Savior, you are adopted by God. You have become a joint-heir with Christ Jesus, His Son! Stop and let that truth sink in. It is vital that you truly grasp and not let go of your identity in Christ. You no longer live. You've been born-again, given a new name, and a new identity. The old life is gone and all things have become new! Memorize 2 Corinthians 5:17 and let it bring you much joy—the joy of the Lord!

## PRAYER

From your heart, write your own prayer(s) below or in a journal.

## FOR REFLECTION AND MEDITATION

### MEMORIZE James 5:16 (NASB)

*"Therefore, confess your sins to one another, and pray for one another so that you may be healed. The effective prayer of a righteous man can accomplish much."*

### MANDATE

*Read 1 Thessalonians 5:16–18 and do the 3 things it tells you to do. Everyday. Every night. You will be amazed what it will do for you!*

### WRITE Your Prayers Here

*(It also helps to write them in a journal and date them. Then you can look back and see how the Lord has answered those prayers.)*

*Notes*

*Chapter Seven*

# TAKING UP YOUR SWORD: HEALING SCRIPTURES

*"May the words of my mouth and the meditation of my heart be acceptable in your sight O LORD, my Rock and my Redeemer."*

*Psalm 19:14 (NLT)*

THE FOLLOWING SCRIPTURES were key to the building up of my faith, enabling me to stand firm and believe the promises God had for me while walking through my cancer trial. I encourage you to feast on these Scriptures. Highlight the ones that jump off the page as you read them; ones that really hit home where you are. Highlight them in your own Bible. Handwrite them on sticky notes and post them on your bathroom mirror, the refrigerator door, the dash of your car, your desk, or the edge of your computer screen. Write them in your journal. Put a list of them in your smartphone and wherever else you will see them daily. Meditate on them day and night (Psalm 1) and most of all, **speak them aloud** daily. All of these exercises help you work the truth of that verse into your heart and life.

Remember, "...*the Word of God is alive and active, sharper than any double-edged sword, it penetrates even to dividing soul and spirit, joints and marrow; it judges the thoughts and attitudes of the heart" (Heb.4:12);* and *"Death and life are in the power of the tongue: and they that love it shall eat the fruit thereof" (Prov.18:21).* Consequently, when you speak the Word (by faith believing) you are speaking life that goes forth like a sharp scalpel in the hands of a skilled physician (*the* Great Physician!) to remove death and "dis-ease" (from our body, mind, *and* spirit) and bring life and peace. Hosea 4:6 is a powerful warning that begins by stating, *"My people are destroyed for lack of knowledge..." John 8:32 says, "You will know the truth, and the truth will make you free."* God's Word is *the* knowledge and *the* truth that brings life and sets you free!

Note that some of the verses are listed more than once in different translations. Occasionally, one translation will bring the original Greek or Hebrew meaning of certain words to life even more than others. Bold type, capitalization and brackets are added unless the verse is the Amplified Version (AMP), in which case, parenthesis are part of the verse and are merely further descriptions from the Greek/Hebrew text. Following the Scripture references are personal notes regarding what that verse meant for me. The Scriptures are listed in successive order so that once you find the first book/chapter/verse listed in your own Bible, you will "keep going right" as you turn to the next book/verse in your Bible. I encourage you to dwell and feast on these Scriptures; continually speaking them over yourself and your circumstances. Just like superfoods that nourish the body and build up its immunity to stave off sickness and disease, so it is with God's Word: it is manna from heaven, the bread of life. His Word will nourish and build up your body, mind, and spirit.

*"And Caleb stilled the people before Moses, and said,* **let us go up at once, and possess it; for we are well able to overcome it."**

*Numbers 13:30 (KJV)*

Just like David when he came up against Goliath, Caleb didn't let the seemingly overwhelming circumstances sway him from God's promises and power to defeat their enemy.

*"...I can't say whatever I please,*
*I must speak only what God puts in my mouth."*
*Numbers 22:38 (NIV)*

It is imperative that we watch the confession of our lips. I refused to say anything that would even imply acceptance of terminal illness or death. I didn't deny that I had cancer, but I most certainly denied its right to remain in my body and usher in death. Instead, I would tell people, "Cancer may have shown up as an unwanted house guest, but it was given notice it can't stay". When I had to tell my family the diagnosis, I added, "Look, I may have cancer but cancer doesn't have me. I belong to Christ and HE has the final say so. And He told me this is not unto death." Death may have come knocking at my door but rather than cower in fear, I answered the door, boldly told death it came to the wrong house, and commanded it to be gone in Jesus' name! We can and must keep our focus and walk in the authority we've been given in Christ.

*"Remember the LORD your God.*
*He is the one who gives you power to be successful, in order to fulfill the*
*covenant He confirmed to your ancestors with an oath."*
*Deuteronomy 8:18 (NLT)*

The word "remember" is key. No matter how you feel: *remember.* *REMEMBER.* **REMEMBER** the one who is in covenant with you by His own blood. He is "I AM" and He is your heavenly Father and Healer. If He is for you, who can defeat you?

*"Be strong and courageous. Do not be afraid or terrified because of them, for*
*the LORD your God goes with you; He will never leave you nor forsake you."*
*Deuteronomy 31:6 (NIV)*

*"The LORD said to me… 'I am watching over My Word to perform it.'"*
*Jeremiah 1:12 (ESV)*

Lay stake to your healing and claim it—it's yours. The deed has been paid in full at Calvary! And He watches over His Word to perform it in the lives of those who will believe.

*"And all these blessings shall come on thee,*
*and overtake thee, if thou shalt hearken unto the*
*voice of the Lord thy God."*
*Deuteronomy 28:2 (KJV)*

Be sensitive to the voice of the Lord. If He points out sin in your life, deal with it. Confess it, repent of it, and keep moving forward by His mercy and grace.

*"David said to Saul, "Let no one lose heart on account of this Philistine*
*(Goliath); your servant will go and fight him."*
*1 Samuel 17:32 (NIV)*

As soon as you take your eyes off God and gaze at the giant—the diagnosis, prognosis, pain, etc.—you're vulnerable to fear, doubt and unbelief. Keep your focus and holdfast to the confession of your faith.

*"David said to the Philistine [Goliath], 'You come against me with*
*sword and spear and javelin, but I come against you in the name of the*
*Lord Almighty, the God of the armies of Israel, whom you have defied.*
*This day the Lord will deliver you into my hands, and I'll strike you*
*down and cut off your head. This very day I will give the carcasses of*
*the Philistine army to the birds and the wild animals, and the whole*
*world will know that there is a God in Israel. All those gathered here*
*will know that it is not by sword or spear that the Lord saves; for the*
*battle is the Lord's, and He will give all of you into our hands.'"*
*1 Samuel 17:45–47 (NIV)*

Make this your battlecry as well!

*"Blessed is the man that walketh not in the counsel of the ungodly, nor
standeth in the way of sinners, nor sitteth in the seat of the scornful.
But his delight is in the law of the Lord; and in His law doth he meditate
day and night. And he shall be like a tree planted by the rivers of water,
that bringeth forth his fruit in his season; his leaf also shall not wither;
and whatsoever he doeth shall prosper."*

*Psalm 1:1–3 (KJV)*

Close your gate to negative talkers or compromising people,
entertainment, distractions, etc. in order to stay the course. This is
war. Surrounding yourself with positive allies is crucial.

*"Oh, the joys of those who do not follow the advice of the wicked, or stand
around with sinners, or join in with mockers.
But they delight in the law of the LORD, meditating on it day and night.
They are like trees planted along the riverbank, bearing fruit each season.
Their leaves never wither, and they prosper in all they do."*

*Psalm 1:1–3 (NLT)*

Stay as far away from people described in the first half of this
verse as possible and surround yourself with the latter. You must be
planted in a life-giving community of believers (ie; church or Bible
study group) as well as in your personal relationship with Jesus and
His Word.

*"Keep your servant from deliberate sins! Don't let them control me.
Then I will be free of guilt and innocent of great sin.
May the words of my mouth and the meditation of my heart
be pleasing to You, O LORD, my Rock and my Redeemer."*

*Psalm 19:13–14 (NLT)*

Don't let satan trip you up. If you struggle with a habitual sin,
continue fighting the good fight against that sin and trust that God
is fighting for you and with you. His mercies are new every morning,

so don't let the enemy tell you otherwise. The Lord promised that a broken and repentant heart would never be despised by Him (Ps.51:17).

> *"But Thou art Holy, O Thou that inhabitest*
> *the praises of Israel."*
> *Psalm 22:3 (KJV)*

One of the most powerful truths we can put into practice in our life is that God literally inhabits the praises of His people! And, according to 2 Corinthians 3:17, ***"...where the Spirit of the Lord is, there is freedom!"*** When you praise the Lord in every circumstance, He shows up in the midst of your praise and powerful things happen in and through you.

> *"The LORD is my Shepherd, I shall not want."*
> *Psalm 23:1 (KJV)*

Boom! There it is! He knows what you need and He's got it covered; so just abide in Him.

> *"The LORD is the strength of my life; of whom shall I be afraid?"*
> *Psalm 27:1 (KJV)*

Often times, in the heat of our trial, we feel we're too weak to carry on. The truth is, we are! But only apart from Christ are we too weak to stand firm. When we holdfast to the truth of Jesus and abide in His presence, we are doing our part. He is the one who fights for us. All we have to do is hold our position of faith in Him and His promises. When you feel you have no strength to continue fighting the good fight, take a time out from the circumstances and get alone with God. Put on some praise and worship music and start thanking Him for being your ever-present help in time of need. Ask Him to breathe new life into you and empower you with His Holy Spirit.

*"Delight thyself in the LORD and*
*He shall give thee the desires of thine heart."*
*Psalm 37:4 (KJV)*

When you boil down the desires of your heart, what's left is the desire for love, joy, peace, safety, comfort, liberty, and happiness for ourselves and those we love. He will give you these desires as you abide/dwell in the shadow of the Almighty God. So cling to Him and let His presence fill your life with "every good and perfect gift" (James 1:17).

*Be still in the presence of the LORD,*
*and wait patiently for Him to act."*
*Psalm 37:7a (NLT)*

Be still. Trust. Abide in His omniscience, omnipotence, and loving arms. He's holding you close; let Him.

*"It is better to be godly and have little than to be evil and rich. For the*
*strength of the wicked will be shattered, but the LORD takes care of the*
*godly. Day by day the LORD takes care of the innocent [righteous], and*
*they will receive an inheritance that lasts forever. They will not be disgraced*
*in hard times; even in famine they will have more than enough."*
*Psalm 37:18 (NLT)*

This was the Word the Lord gave me when my husband lost his job, long before the cancer. He was (and still is) true to His Word. He will not forsake the righteous or leave His children destitute to beg for bread.

*"The LORD directs the steps of the godly.*
***He delights in every detail of their lives***.
*Though they stumble, they will never fall,*
*for **the LORD holds them with His hand**."*
*Psalm 37:23–24 (NLT)*

What a comforting truth! The godly refers to all who have accepted Christ as their Savior and live their lives to honor Him.

*"Create in me a clean heart, O God; and renew a right spirit within me."*
*Psalm 51:10 (KJV)*

I pray this daily. Allow the Lord to search your heart and show you any wicked way in you. Repent of your sin and He is faithful and just to forgive you. Repentance of sin is key to health and healing of our body, mind, and spirit. We simply cannot walk in truth without a repentant heart. We must hate sin and chase after purity in Christ in order to achieve freedom in Christ. As long as we rationalize holding onto something that the Lord is telling us to repent (walk away) from, we will never know the joy and power of Christ in us.

*"You are my strength; I wait for You to rescue me,*
*for You, O God, are my Fortress.*
*In His unfailing love, my God will stand with me.*
*He will let me look down in triumph on all my enemies."*
*Psalm 59:9–10 (NLT)*

Whenever your circumstances feel over your head, remember they're under His feet. And you are *"seated with Christ at the right hand of the Father"* (Eph.2:6).

**"This I declare about the LORD;**
*He alone is my refuge, my place of safety;*
*He is my God and I will trust Him.*
*For He will rescue you [me] from every trap*
*and protect you [me] from deadly disease."*
*Psalm 91:2–3 (NLT)*

Quote this as many times day and night as necessary to remain steadfast in your faith. I always personalize them to make them more meaningful to me.

*"**Bless the Lord, O my soul**, and all that is within me bless His holy name. Bless the Lord, O my soul, and **forget not all His benefits**. Who **forgives** all your iniquities, who **heals** all your diseases, who **redeems** your life from destruction, who **crowns** you with lovingkindness and tender mercies, who **satisfies** your mouth with good things, so that your youth is renewed as the eagle's."*

*Psalm 103:1–5 (NKJV)*

I cannot tell you how many times a day I quote this—but it's a lot! I often quote this when praising the Lord and when I need to remind myself of His power, goodness, and promises in my life.

*"He also brought them out with silver and gold,*
*and there was none feeble among them."*

*Psalm 105:37 (KJV)*

*"He sent His Word and healed them,*
*and delivered them from all their destructions."*

*Psalm 107:20 (NKJV)*

Thank you, Jesus!

*"Oh that men would **give thanks to the Lord for His goodness**, and **for His wonderful works** to the children of men! Let them **sacrifice the sacrifices of thanksgiving**, and **declare His works** with rejoicing."*

*Psalm 107:22 (NKJV)*

There is so much power in praising the Lord for all His goodness and wonderful works. Burdens lift off our shoulders when we praise Him because it renews our mind—getting our thoughts off the size of our problems and onto the size of our God! Never forget what He has done for you—He has saved your soul from destruction and written your name in the Lamb's Book of Life! If that's all He ever does for you, it's enough to give thanks everyday for all eternity!

> *"Oh, God…Give us help from trouble, for the help of man is useless.*
> **Through God we WILL do valiantly,**
> *for it is He who shall tread down our enemies."*
> *Psalm 109:12–13 (NKJV)*

I declare the second part of this verse (aloud!) with confidence until it reaches deep in my spirit and empowers me to stand firm and believe. When we believe, obey, and abide in Him, He WILL work valiantly on our behalf.

> *"I shall not die, but live and declare the works of the LORD."*
> *Psalm 118:17 (KJV)*

If I said this once, I said it 10,000 times while fighting cancer. Many times, in my weakest moments, this was the only Scripture I could even think to quote.

> *"This is my comfort in my affliction, for*
> *Your Word has given me life."*
> *Psalm 119:50 (NKJV)*

I am a living testament to this! All who are born-again are testaments to this!

> *"Unless Your law had been my delight,*
> *I would then have perished in my affliction.*
> *I will never forget your precepts,*
> *for by them, You have given me life."*
> *Psalm 119:92–93 (NKJV)*

> *"Thy Word is a lamp unto my feet and a light unto my path."*
> *Psalm 119:105 (KJV)*

> *"I am afflicted very much; Revive me, O LORD, according to Your Word."*
> *Psalm 119:107 (NKJV)*

*"You are my hiding place and my shield;*
*I hope in Your Word."*
*Psalm 119:114 (NKJV)*

Let Him hide you under the shadow of his wing (Psalm 91) like a mother bird would shelter her frail baby. He knows how frail you are and longs to comfort and protect you.

*"You are near, O LORD, and all Your commandments are truth."*
*Psalm 119:151 (NKJV)*

*"Consider my affliction and deliver me, for I do not forget Your law.*
*Plead my cause and redeem me;*
**Revive me according to Your Word."**
*Psalm 119:153–154 (NKJV)*

*"My son [daughter], do not forget My teaching,*
*but* **keep My commands in your heart,**
*for they will prolong your life many years*
*and bring you peace and prosperity."*
*Proverbs 3:1–2 (NIV)*

*"Trust in the Lord with all your heart*
*and lean not on your own understanding;*
*in all your ways* **submit to Him,**
*and He will make your paths straight.*
**Do not be wise in your own eyes;**
**fear the Lord** *and* **shun evil.**
**This will bring health** *to your body*
*and nourishment to your bones.*
*Honor the Lord with your wealth,*
*with the firstfruits of all your crops;*
*then your barns will be filled to overflowing,*
*and your vats will brim over with new wine."*
*Proverbs 3:5–10 (NIV)*

**"Blessed are those who find wisdom**, *those who gain under-standing, for she is more profitable than silver and yields better returns than gold. She is more precious than rubies; nothing you desire can compare with her. Long life is in her right hand; in her left hand are riches and honor. Her ways are pleasant ways, and all her paths are peace.* **She is a tree of life to those who take hold of her**; *those who holdfast to her will be blessed."*

*Proverbs 3:13–18 (NIV)*

*"My son, give attention to My Words, incline your ear to My sayings. Do not let them depart from your eyes; keep them in the midst of your heart;* **for they are life to those who find them and health to all their flesh.**"

*Proverbs 4:20–22 (NIV)*

This passage is key to our success in Christ. We must keep the truth of His Word in our ears (what we listen to), in our eyes (what we look at/watch) and in the midst of our hearts (what we allow our minds to dwell on and our hearts to believe). Everything we do and say either draws us closer to Christ or further from Him. Choose wisely.

*"The blessing of the Lord, it maketh rich, and He addeth no sorrow with it."*
*Proverbs 10:22 (KJV)*

Whether we have financial wealth, physical health, or not, when we have the blessing of the Holy Spirit in our lives (producing the fruit of the Holy Spirit in us) we are truly rich!

*"Roll your works upon the Lord*
*(commit and trust them wholly to Him;*
*He will cause your thoughts to become agreeable to His will, and)*
*so shall your plans be established and succeed."*

*Proverbs 16:3 (AMP)*

*"Fear thou not! For I am with thee:*
*be not dismayed for I am thy God.*
*I WILL strengthen thee; yea,*
*I WILL uphold thee; yea,*
*I WILL help thee: yea,*
*I WILL uphold thee*
*with the right hand of My righteousness."*
*Isaiah 41:10 (KJV)*

You definitely want to memorize this Scripture. Whenever fear strikes your heart, quote this until the fear leaves. That is putting into practice the scripture that tells us to resist the devil and he will flee from you (James 4:7). Remember, fear isn't just an emotion, it's a spirit that will attack us to derail our faith (2 Tim. 1:7).

*"He was wounded for our transgressions,*
*He was bruised for our iniquities;*
*the chastisement of our peace was upon Him,*
*and by His stripes we are healed."*
*Isaiah 53:5 (KJV)*

This may be the most powerful verse in all the Bible! He made a way for us—*He* bore the penalty, we reap the benefits! Praise God!

**"In the beginning was the Word,**
**and the Word was with God**
**and the Word was God**
**and the Word became flesh**
**and dwelt among us.**
**[And that flesh] was wounded for our transgressions,**
**He was bruised for our iniquities;**
**The chastisement for our peace was upon him,**
**AND BY HIS STRIPES WE ARE HEALED."**
*John 1:1,14; Isaiah 53:5 (KJV)*

These were foundational scriptures for me to step out in faith and believe for my healing. I quoted these passages of scripture countless times throughout my battle to keep my faith strong.

*"It was our weaknesses He carried;*
*it was our sorrows that weighed Him down.*
*And we thought His troubles were a punishment from God,*
*a punishment for His own sins!*
*But He was pierced for our rebellion,*
*crushed for our sins.*
*But He was beaten so we could be whole.*
*He was whipped so we could be healed. "*
*Isaiah 53:4–5 (NLT)*

What an incredibly loving, selfless God. This passage always caused a tenacious fight to rise up within me. Knowing what my God and Savior suffered for *my* healing made me all the more determined to fight the fight of faith that He may receive the glory due His name.

*"'In a little wrath I hid My face from thee for a moment; but with*
*everlasting kindness will I have mercy on thee,' saith the Lord*
*thy Redeemer…'No weapon that is formed against thee shall prosper;*
*and every tongue that shall rise against thee in judgment thou shalt condemn.*
*This is the heritage of the servants of the Lord,*
*and their righteousness is of Me,' saith the Lord."*
*Isaiah 54:8, 17 (KJV)*

Whose report are you going to believe (Isaiah 53:1–5)? What the Holy Spirit has quickened in your heart according to His Word or the report of the enemy of your soul?

*"O LORD, my strength, and my stronghold;*
*and my refuge in the day of affliction."*
*Jeremiah 16:19 (KJV)*

*"For I will restore life to you*
*and heal you of your wounds, says the Lord."*
*Jeremiah 30:17 (NKJV)*

Believe it! He longs to show you His mighty love and power. Stand in front of the mirror and speak this verse over yourself; however many times as necessary until it bursts forth in your heart and life!

*"'Bring ye all the tithes into the storehouse,*
*that there may be meat in Mine house,*
*and **prove Me now** herewith,' saith the Lord of hosts,*
*'if I will not open you the windows of heaven, and pour you out*
*a blessing, that there shall not be room enough to receive it.*
***And I will rebuke the devourer for your sakes,***
*and he shall not destroy the fruits of your ground;*
*neither shall your vine cast her fruit before the time in the field,'*
*saith the Lord of hosts.'"*
*Malachi 3:10–11 (KJV)*

This is a command with a promise. When we give at least ten percent (that's what "tithe" means) of our income to God, He promises to bless, protect, and multiply the other ninety percent. I'll never be able to figure out how this works but it has never failed to work in my life. You cannot outgive God! I realize this is the old covenant but when God gives a command *with a promise,* I think it's worth paying attention to. And besides, the new covenant says that it *all* belongs to God! That should be the attitude of our hearts: "Lord, everything I have belongs to You and I give whatever You ask me to give, wherever You ask me to give it—with a cheerful attitude".

*"And I will give unto you the keys of the kingdom of heaven:*
*and whatsoever thou shalt bind on earth shall be bound in heaven:*
*and whatsoever thou shalt loose on earth shall be loosed in heaven."*
*Matthew 16:19 (KJV)*

Just camp right here for awhile. This is amazing! He has given His children this power and authority to use, not just to put on a shelf and admire its concept from afar. Bind up cancer (or whatever you're facing) in the name of Jesus and loose His healing virtue to flow through your body! Bind the lies of the enemy and loose the Spirit of truth to take dominion in your life. You've been given the keys of the kingdom of Heaven—so use them to loose the chains of fear, sickness, addiction, disease, poverty, etc. that hold you in bondage and begin to walk in the freedom that Christ paid for at Calvary.

*"So Jesus said to them, 'Because you have so little faith.*
*Truly I tell you, if you have faith as small as a mustard seed,*
*you can say to this mountain, "Move from here to there,"*
*and it will move. Nothing will be impossible for you.'"*
*Matthew 17:20 (NIV)*

Speak with authority to the mountain in your life that's standing in your way to health and freedom, and command it to be removed. That mountain may be an eating disorder, negative/destructive thoughts, etc. Remember, you stand in Christ's authority not your own. It's His authority in you that causes the mountains to obey your command. And by the power of the Holy Spirit, you are freed to walk in obedience to His will and the benefits of His promises.

*"In the morning, as they went along,*
*they saw the fig tree withered from the roots.*
*Peter remembered and said to Jesus,*
*'Rabbi, look! The fig tree you cursed has withered!'*
*'HAVE FAITH IN GOD' Jesus answered."*
*Mark 11:20–22 (AMP)*

*"So Jesus answered and saith unto them,*
*"HAVE FAITH IN GOD.*
*For assuredly I say unto thee,*
*whosoever shall say unto this mountain,*

*"Be thou removed and be thou cast into the sea"*
*and shall not doubt in his heart,*
*but shall believe that those things which He saith shall come to pass;*
*he shall have whatsoever he saith."*

Mark 11:22–24(KJV)

*"'Have faith in God,' Jesus answered.*
*'Truly I tell you, if anyone says to this mountain, "Go, throw yourself into*
*the sea", and does not doubt in their heart but believes that what they say*
*will happen, it will be done for them. Therefore I tell you, whatever you*
*ask for in prayer, believe that you have received it, and it will be yours. And*
*when you stand praying, if you hold anything against anyone, forgive them,*
*so that your Father in heaven may forgive you your sins.'"*

Mark 11:22–25 (NIV)

Doubt and unforgiveness will hinder the power of God in your life, so get rid of them now.

*"Look, I have given you authority over ALL the power of the enemy,*
*and you can walk among snakes and scorpions and crush them.*
*Nothing will injure you.*
*But don't rejoice because evil spirits obey you;*
*rejoice because your names are registered in heaven."*

Luke 10:19–20 (NLT)

Did you catch that? Jesus said this to His disciples. All of His disciples through all time and eternity! We have been given all authority over all the power of the enemy (Mark 16:17). Just keep it in perspective; it doesn't even begin to compare to the blessing that our names are written in the Lamb's Book of Life!

*"The thief cometh not, but for to steal, and to kill and to destroy:*
*I [Jesus] am come that they [that's us] might have life*
*and have it more abundantly."*

John 10:10 (KJV)

The life of a man/woman who abides in Christ is more exciting than what anyone else can or will ever experience!

*"As it is written: 'I have made you (Abraham) a father of many nations.'*
*He is our father in the sight of God, in whom he believed—THAT GOD*
*WHO GIVES LIFE TO THE DEAD AND CALLS INTO BEING*
*THINGS THAT WERE NOT."*

*Romans 4:17 (NIV)*

*"..God..who gives life to the dead and speaks of the nonexistent things that*
*(He has foretold and promised) as if they (already) existed."*
*Romans 4:17 (AMP) (c.f. Genesis 17:5)*

I love this verse! We must be eternal-minded. He promised and foretold that you can do all things through Christ, who gives you strength. HE gives life to the dead!

*"As it is written, I have made thee (Abraham) a father of many nations,*
*before Him whom he believed,*
*EVEN GOD, WHO QUICKENETH THE DEAD,*
*AND CALLETH THOSE THINGS WHICH BE NOT*
*AS THOUGH THEY WERE.*
***Who against hope believed in hope,***
*that he might become the father of many nations;*
*according to that which was spoken, so shall thy seed be.*
*And being not weak in faith, he considered not his own body now dead,*
*when he was about an hundred years old,*
*neither yet the deadness of Sarah's womb:*
*HE STAGGERED NOT AT THE PROMISE OF GOD THROUGH*
*UNBELIEF; BUT WAS STRONG IN FAITH, GIVING GLORY*
*TO GOD, AND BEING FULLY PERSUADED THAT, WHAT HE*
*HAD PROMISED, HE WAS ABLE ALSO TO PERFORM.*
*And **therefore it was imputed to him for righteousness**.*
*Now it was not written for his sake alone, that it was imputed to him;*
*But for us also, to whom it shall be imputed,*

*if we believe on Him that raised up Jesus our Lord from the dead;*
*Who was delivered for our offences*
*and was raised again for our justification."*
Romans 4:17–25 (KJV)

Are you really fully persuaded? Do you believe the Word of God or don't you? If so, begin declaring it out loud over your life. Don't dwell on your present circumstances, dwell on His Word. The more you do this, the stronger your faith will become. Your thoughts become the words you speak. Let your thoughts and your words give life and strength to the Word of God not the giants of negativity, fear and faithlessness.

*"For if because of one man's trespass (lapse; offense)*
*death reigned through that one,*
*much more surely will* **those who receive**
**(God's) overflowing grace (unmerited favor)**
**and the free gift of righteousness**
*(putting them into right standing with Himself)*
**reign as kings in life through the one Man,**
**Jesus Christ** *(the Messiah, the Anointed One)."*
Romans 5:17 (AMP)

This is incredible! No matter who you are or what you've done in your past, when you are born-again, you are royalty in Christ Jesus. Start thinking and behaving like the "joint-heir with Christ" that you are (Romans 8:17). Just as kings and queens understand their position of authority and walk in it, so you are to do the same spiritually. Yes, we face many afflictions and "share in His sufferings in order that we may also share in His glory". But regardless the suffering, victory is ours in Christ because His sacrifice has guaranteed our victory over death, hell, and the grave.

*"And so, dear brothers and sisters,*
*I plead with you to give your bodies to God*

*because of all He has done for you.*
*Let them be a living and holy sacrifice—the kind He will find acceptable.*
**This is truly the way to worship Him.**
**Don't copy the behavior and customs of this world,**
**but let God transform you into a new person**
**by changing the way you think.**
**Then you will learn to know God's will for you,**
**which is good and pleasing and perfect."**
*Romans 12:1–2 (NLT)*

Memorize this scripture. Work this truth deep into your heart and mind because however you *think*, your behavior follows suit.

*"Never lag in zeal and in earnest endeavor;*
*be aglow and burning with the Spirit, serving the Lord.*
*Rejoice and exult in hope; be steadfast and patient in suffering*
*and tribulation; be constant in prayer."*
*Romans 12:11–12 (AMP)*

The first key to remaining zealous and earnestly endeavoring is to daily abide in His presence. The second, and equally important key, is to obey Him. What is He asking you to do? Do it and spiritual breakthrough will follow!

*"And God is able to make all grace abound toward you,*
*that ye, always having all sufficiency in all things,*
*may abound to every good work:*
*(As it is written, He hath dispersed abroad;*
*He hath given to the poor:*
*His righteousness remaineth forever.)"*
*2 Corinthians 9:8–9 (KJV)*

We are without excuse because HE has freely given us all the grace we need to be more than conquerors in Christ Jesus. How's that for good news?!

*"...you have heard about Him and were taught in Him,*
*as the Truth is in Jesus, to put off your old self,*
*which belongs to your former manner of life*
*and is corrupt through deceitful desires,*
*and to BE RENEWED IN THE SPIRIT OF YOUR MINDS,*
*AND TO PUT ON THE NEW SELF,*
*CREATED AFTER THE LIKENESS OF GOD*
*IN TRUE RIGHTEOUSNESS AND HOLINESS.*
*PUT OFF FALSEHOOD..SPEAK THE TRUTH..*
*(THAT BY HIS STRIPES YOU ARE HEALED!)"*

*Ephesians 4:20–25(ESV)*

Your mind is renewed by the Word of God, therefore, refuse to allow thoughts of sickness, lack, failure, and/or defeat inhabit your mind.

*"..**Be strong in the Lord and in His mighty power**.*
***Put on all of God's armor** so that you will be able to stand firm*
*against all strategies of the devil.*
***For we are not fighting against flesh-and-blood enemies,***
***but against evil rulers and authorities of the unseen***
***world, against mighty powers in this dark world,***
***and against evil spirits in the heavenly places.***
*Therefore, **put on every piece of God's armor***
*so you will be able to resist the enemy in the time of evil.*
*Then after the battle you will still be standing firm.*
***Stand your ground, putting on the belt of truth***
*and **the body armor of God's righteousness**.*
*For shoes, **put on the peace that comes from the Good***
***News** so that you will **be fully prepared**.*
*In addition to all of these, **hold up the shield of faith***
*to stop the fiery arrows of the devil.*
***Put on salvation as your helmet**, and*
***take the sword of the Spirit, which is the Word of God.***

**Pray in the Spirit at all times** *and on every occasion.*
**Stay alert** *and* **be persistent** *in your prayers*
*for all believers everywhere.*
*Ephesians 6:10–18 (NLT)*

Go back and read just the bold print of this passage. Do you see the seriousness and urgent command of your commanding officer here? This is war. You are in a battle. Like any competent soldier on the battlefield, you must stay alert to any sneak attack of the enemy. You must be armed and ready at all times. We must keep our focus. It's so easy to get discouraged when we are physically or emotionally ill. Like Peter walking on the water, we cannot get distracted by our circumstances or they will consume us—we must keep our focus on Jesus, our Healer and Deliverer.

*We lack nothing for… "my God shall supply all your [my] needs*
*according to His riches in glory by Christ Jesus."*
*Philippians 4:19 (KJV)*

*"Let us hold fast the confession of our hope without wavering,*
*for He who promised is Faithful."*
*Hebrews 10:23 (ESV)*

I keep this Scripture taped to my bathroom mirror so that I see it every morning and every evening. We must stand firm in our belief no matter how strongly the storm rages. Tenacious faith is warfare and yields powerful rewards.

*"Submit yourselves, then, to God.*
*Resist the devil,*
*and he will flee from you."*
*James 4:7 (NIV)*

Satan will do everything he can to derail your faith. We must resist his fiery darts of doubt, discouragement, anger, resentment, fear, depression, apathy, etc. Hold up your shield of faith against these onslaughts and wield your weapon, the Word of God, at the enemy's attack.

> *"His divine power has granted to us all things*
> *that pertain to life and godliness,*
> *through the knowledge of Him who called us*
> *to His own glory and excellence,*
> **by which He has granted to us**
> **His precious and very great promises,**
> *so that through them*
> **you may become partakers of the divine nature,**
> *having escaped from the corruption*
> *that is in the world because of sinful desire."*
> 2 *Peter 1:2–4 (KJV)*

## LET THE WEAK SAY, "I AM STRONG!"

These scriptures possess the power to radically change your life and the lives of those in your world, **if** you choose to grab hold of them and work them into your heart and life. My father, like all of us, was far from perfect, but the greatest gift he gave me was that he taught me to go into my "prayer closet" (that was my bedside as a child), fall to my knees in prayer, and not to get up until I experienced the power of God made manifest in my heart. He modeled that in our home and in our church. He and my mother modeled hearts that were in love with Jesus and lives built on the truths of God's Word. We read the Bible every morning before school and each of us took our turn praying before we ever stepped foot into our day. I knew my parents loved the LORD with everything in them and they poured that love onto my sisters and me.

My maternal grandfather was a homeless teenager who found refuge in a godly woman's home. He had nothing to do with God but every morning before he left for work, this elderly woman would make him kneel down as she would lay her hands on his head and pray for him. As an adult, he was a mean, rough logger in the mountains of Oregon. My mother recalls his coming home from work one night and sitting down to a family dinner with a broken nose from having been in a brawl. But the prayers of that elderly woman had taken root. The truths she spoke into my grandfather's heart eventually came to fruition when my mother was a little girl. My grandfather went on to accept Christ, fall madly in love with Jesus, and become a bi-vocational pastor. I never knew the mean, rough, godless man she said he was before Christ changed his life. All I knew, was a Papa who was so in love with Jesus that tears would fill his eyes as he would randomly burst into song about his wonderful Savior. I remember him as a man who was so joyful all the time and always talking about the goodness of God.

My father's father was not a believer until he was old and retired. But my father's mother was a woman of prayer and great faith. She raised all seven of her children in the truth of God's Word. Her faithfulness to God set into motion one of the most impactful families for God on the west coast during that era. All 7 of her children went into ministry of some sort and many of her grandchildren and great-grandchildren have done the same. Hundreds of churches have been planted all over the world through her children and grandchildren. Only when we get to heaven will we know the countless souls that were impacted by this family because of one mother who had a personal relationship with God through the truths of His Word and the power of His Holy Spirit!

Because my grandparents and parents chose to live a life of tenacious faith, I am here today as a living miracle to bring the hope of the world—Jesus—to all who will hear. Pick up your sword soldier! March into battle with the Sword of the Spirit (the Word of God) in your hand and His high praises on your lips. No matter how weak you feel, remember, **it's not your strength that yields victory, it's His.** All you have to do is take hold of the Word and stand firm.

When I was in horrible pain and so weak from chemo, many times all I had was a tearful whisper. But I used that whisper to speak the Word of God over myself. Whether it's a whisper or a shout, when His Word comes forth, it comes forth in immeasurable, unstoppable power that ripples throughout all time and eternity.

You may not have had a father like mine (neither did my father!), but you now hold these truths in your hand. I implore you, start today implementing these powerful truths and tools into your daily life. You will be changing your destiny and the destiny for countless souls that come after you. Come up higher and *abide* in the shadow of the Almighty God. When you do, you will be opening the door to the supernatural truths and power of God, the great I AM, and allowing Him to come in and rock your world with "*...joy that is indescribable and full of glory!*"

*"My thoughts are nothing like your thoughts," says the LORD.*
*"And My ways are far beyond anything you could imagine.*
*For just as the heavens are higher than the earth,*
*So My ways are higher than your ways*
*and My thoughts higher than your thoughts."*

*"The rain and snow come down from the heavens*
*and stay on the ground to water the earth.*
*They cause the grain to grow,*
*producing seed for the farmer and bread for the hungry.*
*It is the same with My Word.*
*I send it out, and it always produces fruit.*
*It will accomplish all I want it to,*
*And it will prosper everywhere I send it.*

*You will live in joy and peace.*
*The mountains and the hills will burst into song,*
*And the trees of the field will clap their hands!*
*Where once there were thorns, cypress trees will grow.*
*Where nettles grew, myrtles will sprout up.*
*These events will bring great honor to the LORD's name;*
*They will be an everlasting sign of His power and love."*
Isaiah 55:8–13

## PRAYER

"Oh God, I thank You for Your Word! Thank You that it is *"...alive and active and sharper than any double-edged sword"* (including a scalpel!). Thank You that every promise in the Word is *"yes!"* for those who are in Christ Jesus—that's me! Your Word is a lamp to my feet, giving me guidance. Your Word is truth and it sets me free. Your Word is a mighty fortress to those that believe. Thank You for Your Holy Spirit that breathes life and revelation upon me as I study Your Word. I love Your Word for by its precepts, I am transformed and renewed. I love You, LORD, more than life itself. Amen!"

## FOR REFLECTION AND MEDITATION

### MEMORIZE John 15:7-8 and Psalm 19:14

*"If you abide in Me and My words abide in you, you will ask what you desire, and it shall be done for you. By this is My Father glorified, that you bear much fruit; and so prove to be My disciples." John 15:7–8 (NHEB)*

*"May the words of my mouth and the meditation of my heart be acceptable in your sight O LORD, my Rock and my Redeemer." Psalm 19:14 (NLT)*

### MEDITATE

*Type or write out Ephesians 6:12–19, Hebrews 4:12, and Proverbs 18:21. Post it anywhere and everywhere you will see it throughout the day and night (including in your smartphone!) and quote/declare them out loud.*

### MANDATE

*Praying scripture (aloud) is powerful! Start with the Lord's prayer. It's a great prayer and a great outline for extended praying. Then write your own prayers using scriptures that pertain to your personal situation.*

*Notes*

# SUGGESTED READING

***God's Creative Power for Healing***
  Charles Capps (Capps Publishing)

***Healed of Cancer***
  Dodie Osteen (John Osteen Publications)

***A Woman's Guide to Spirit-Filled Living***
  Quinn Sherrer and Ruthanne Garlock (Chosen Books
  Publishing)

***Ever Increasing Faith***
  Smith Wigglesworth (CreateSpace Independent Publishing)

***Future Grace***
  John Piper (Multnomah Publishing)

***Heaven***
  Randy Alcorn (Tyndale Momentum Publishing)

***Learn The Bible in 24 Hours***
  Dr. Chuck Missler (Thomas Nelson Publishing)

***Boundaries***
  Dr. Henry Cloud & Dr. John Townsend (Zondervan
  Publishing)

***Guidelines for Maximized Health: The Power of Faith
and Medicine"***
  Dr. Leslie Bostick (Faith One Publishing)

# About the Author

SALLI MELILLI IS a licensed minister and life coach, author and speaker. She is also a worship leader and voice instructor with a demonstrated history of working in the professional training and coaching industry. Salli has sung professionally for many years, appearing on several worldwide Christians broadcasts. Her testimony of healing has been featured in numerous published articles and television programs, including the 700 Club. She and her husband reside in California near their two grown children.

# Contact and Booking

If you would like to book Salli Melilli to speak at your corporation, church, or conference, please contact us at salli@divinemiracle.org. For more contact information, articles, inspiration, and products, visit our website at divinemiracle.org.

Made in the USA
Las Vegas, NV
10 June 2021